COUNTRIES OF THE WORLD

The Philippines

Gareth Stevens Publishing
A WORLD ALMANAC EDUCATION GROUP COMPANY

About the Author: Joaquin L. Gonzalez III
has a doctorate in political science and has
written extensively on the Philippines and
the Asia-Pacific. A professional educator and
administrator, he has taught in the United
States, Singapore, and the Philippines.

PICTURE CREDITS
Agence de Presse ANA: 5 (top), 9 (bottom),
    18 (top)
Archive Photos: 5 (bottom), 12 (top), 13, 15
    (top), 16, 37 (top), 60, 75, 77, 78, 80, 84
Bes Stock: cover, 3 (center), 27, 34, 39
    (bottom), 62, 63
Bong Cayabyab: 81
Bruce Coleman Collection: 53
Christine Osborne Pictures: 39 (top), 40, 50
Victor Englebert: 3 (bottom), 21, 22, 23, 24,
    25, 26, 33, 35, 36, 37 (bottom), 41, 46,
    58, 59, 64, 69, 79, 87
Ayesha C. Ercelawn: 29 (bottom), 71, 82,
    85, 91
Filipinas Heritage Library: 56 (bottom), 57
Focus Team — Italy: 7, 66, 73
Haga Library, Japan: 1
HBL Network Photo Agency: 6, 15 (center
    and bottom), 18 (bottom), 54, 68, 74
The Hutchison Library: 14 (bottom), 76
Earl Kowall: 20, 48, 49, 72
Lopez Memorial Foundation: 56 (top)
North Wind Picture Archives: 10, 11
Philippine Department of Tourism —
    Singapore Office: 2, 8, 9 (top), 31, 42, 52
    (top and bottom), 67
Pietro Scòzzari: 12 (bottom), 32, 38, 89
George C. Tapan: 65
Lauren C. Te: 83
Topham Picturepoint: 3 (top), 4, 19, 29
    (top), 30, 47, 51, 55
Travel Ink Photo and Feature Library: 17
Trip Photo Library: 14 (top), 28, 43, 44, 45,
    61, 70

Digital Scanning by Superskill Graphics Pte Ltd

Written by
JOAQUIN L. GONZALEZ III

Edited by
SELINA KUO

Designed by
LYNN CHIN

Picture research by
SUSAN JANE MANUEL

First published in North America in 2001 by
Gareth Stevens Publishing
A World Almanac Education Group Company
330 West Olive Street, Suite 100
Milwaukee, Wisconsin 53212 USA

For a free color catalog describing
Gareth Stevens' list of high-quality books
and multimedia programs, call
1-800-542-2595 (USA) or
1-800-461-9120 (CANADA).
Gareth Stevens Publishing's
Fax: (414) 332-3567.

© **TIMES MEDIA PRIVATE LIMITED 2001**
Originated and designed by
Times Editions
An imprint of Times Media Private Limited
A member of the Times Publishing Group
Times Centre, 1 New Industrial Road
Singapore 536196
http://www.timesone.com.sg/te

Library of Congress Cataloging-in-Publication Data available upon
request from publisher. Fax: (414) 336-0157 for the attention of the
Publishing Records Department.

ISBN 0-8368-2334-6

Printed in Malaysia

1 2 3 4 5 6 7 8 9 05 04 03 02 01

Contents

4

AN OVERVIEW OF THE PHILIPPINES

Nicknamed *Pearl of the Orient Seas*, the Philippines is an archipelago of more than 7,100 islands. The country is the only predominantly Christian nation in Asia. From the thirteenth to the fifteenth centuries, the islands attracted merchants from China, India, the Middle East, and Southeast Asia. In 1521, the first Spaniards arrived. The Philippines was controlled by Spain for 333 years (1565–1898), the United States for forty-six years, and Japan for three years. Throughout this time of foreign rule, Filipinos fought bravely against the occupying powers. On July 4, 1946, the Philippines became one of the first countries in Asia to gain independence from foreign control. Today, the Philippines is a free and democratic nation.

Opposite: **Mount Isarog on Luzon is one of many dormant volcanoes in the Philippines. Many Filipinos live near it because its lower slopes are fertile.**

Below: **Due to the influence of Roman Catholicism, Philippine children are seen as a blessing from God.**

THE FLAG OF THE PHILIPPINES

The current Philippine flag is a composite of various flags and banners used in the revolution against Spanish rule. The white equilateral triangle stands for the equality of all people. Each of the three stars represents approximately one third of the Philippine Archipelago — Luzon in the north, Mindanao in the south, and the group of islands in between them called the Visayas. The eight rays of the sun stand for the eight provinces that started the revolt against Spain. The blue stripe symbolizes the unity of the Filipinos and their love of peace, and the red stripe symbolizes courage and loyalty to the country.

Geography

Land and Water

Located in Southeast Asia, between the equator and the Tropic of Cancer, the Philippine Archipelago is surrounded by large bodies of water — the Philippine Sea to the east, the South China Sea to the west, the Bashi Channel to the north, and the Sulu and Celebes seas to the south. The islands lie between the southern tip of Taiwan and the northern parts of Borneo and Indonesia. Covering an area of 115,830 square miles (300,000 square kilometers), the Philippines is larger than the United Kingdom but slightly smaller than Japan. The country has about 7,107 islands. Of these, only 2,773 have names and 1,190 are inhabited.

At 22,549 miles (36,289 km), the Philippines has the longest discontinuous coastline in the world. Its seacoasts are dotted with bays and gulfs, creating some of the world's finest harbors. Manila Bay, with a coastline of more than 100 miles (161 km) and an approximate area of 770 square miles (1,994 square km), is the largest bay in the Philippines and also one of Asia's best harbors.

Below: **Two Filipinos spend a leisurely afternoon on the beach on the island of Bohol.**

The Philippines' most rugged mountain area is on the island of Luzon. The country has a total of seven major mountain ranges. Among these, the most important are the Sierra Madre and the Cordillera Central. At 9,692 feet (2,954 meters), Mount Apo is the country's tallest peak and is located on the main southern island of Mindanao. One of the Philippines' most unusual natural land formations is the Chocolate Hills on the island of Bohol. There are 1,776 of these uniformly shaped hills, and their heights range from 131 to 394 feet (40 to 120 m).

Of the many Philippine gulfs, the better known are Lingayen Gulf, Leyte Gulf, and Davao Gulf. Laguna de Bay in Laguna province is one of the country's largest lakes. Lake Taal in Batangas province, however, attracts more visitors because Taal Volcano is situated in the middle of the lake, which is itself the crater lake of a larger volcano. Pulangi, also known as the Rio Grande Mindanao, is the country's longest river. It flows for approximately 200 miles (320 km) through western Mindanao. Pagsanjan Falls on Luzon and Maria Cristina Falls on Mindanao are two of the country's many picturesque waterfalls.

Above: **The mysterious Chocolate Hills are found on Bohol. Legend has it that they are the tears of a giant who was crying over lost love.**

LAND OF VOLCANOES

About fifty volcanoes are scattered throughout the Philippines. Only ten of them, however, are known to be active.

(*A Closer Look*, page 60)

Dry and Wet Seasons

The Philippine climate is tropical and monsoonal in character. The country has two seasons — the dry season from December to May and the wet season from June to November. The level of humidity remains high even during the dry season, ranging from 71 to 85 percent. The Philippines experiences such humidity partly because it is located in the tropics. Also, water is constantly evaporating from the surrounding ocean and seas, causing the air to be saturated with an uncomfortable moistness. Philippine monsoon seasons last from November to April in the northeast and from May to October in the southwest. The coolest period is from September to November, while the hottest months are April and May. An average of fifteen typhoons a year hits the Philippines. Some of these storms last for days and cause severe destruction with their strong winds and heavy rain.

Left: **Plants and animals at Lake Taal experience the constant tremors of the active Taal Volcano in the lake's center. They also experience harsh weather conditions brought by the many typhoons that blow through the Philippines each year.**

Plants and Animals

The Philippines is home to one of the largest plant and animal communities in the world. With highly fertile soil and warm tropical sunshine throughout the year, the Philippines produces, among other crops, a dazzling array of delicious exotic fruits, including pineapples, mangoes, chicos, durians, and mangosteens. Bananas, in particular, come in about fifty different types! Vast forests are another enviable resource. If properly managed, these forests are capable of replenishing themselves. Narra, a hard wood, and nipa palm are used to build houses. Other natural materials, such as bamboo and rattan, are used to make furniture. Philippine forests are also home to animals such as hogs, deer, goats, and monkeys. Commonly sighted birds in the Philippines include jungle fowl (*Gallus bankiva*), large hornbills, and fruit-pigeons. A wide range of fish and crustaceans, or sea animals that have hard shells covering their bodies, are found in Philippine waters. Large quantities of crabs, shrimp, oysters, tuna, salmon, marlin, halibut, and swordfish are harvested each year.

History

Crossing Bridges and Oceans

The Philippine Archipelago surfaced as a result of violent underwater earthquakes and volcanic activity that took place over one million years ago. Evidence of human existence on the Philippine islands dates back some twenty-two thousand years. Records show that a thriving civilization existed long before the first Europeans arrived. These natives, the Negritos, were later joined by migrating Malays and Indonesians. While some of these migrants walked the "land bridges" that once connected the Philippine islands to the Malay peninsula and the Indonesian Archipelago, others came by sea. These early Asian settlers hunted, fished, and planted for a living. By the 1400s, they were trading with China, India, and the Middle East. The early Philippine population soon became a melting pot of cultures when the foreign traders and the locals began intermarrying.

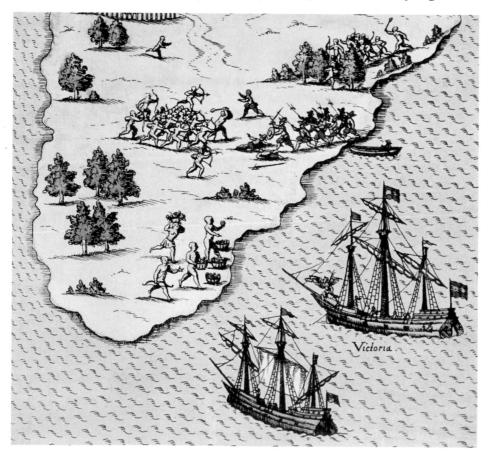

Left: This drawing is an artist's impression of explorer Ferdinand Magellan's landing at Mactan, where he was ultimately killed. Before Mactan, Magellan had made history when he reached Cebu in 1521. He was the first Spanish representative to set foot on any of the Philippine islands. Today, the island of Cebu, like Bohol, is a Philippine province.

Spanish Conquest

Ferdinand Magellan, a Portuguese explorer, led an expedition for Spain that "discovered" the Philippine islands in March 1521. The archipelago was later named "the Philippines" as a tribute to King Philip II, who ruled Spain for much of the sixteenth century. Magellan was slain in a battle with Lapu-Lapu, a fierce local chieftain, before he could return to Spain. The Spanish authorities were undeterred by Magellan's death and established their first permanent settlement on Cebu in 1565. The Spaniards proceeded to unite the islands, controlling them under a central government in Manila, and they introduced Christianity to the natives. The Spanish government and the Catholic Church soon became powerful institutions in the Philippines. The Spanish conquerors and religious orders, however, were unpopular with the locals because they abused their power and treated the Filipinos unfairly. Philippine intellectuals such as José P. Rizal, Marcelo H. del Pilar, Andres Bonifacio, Antonio Luna, and Mariano Ponce made requests for serious reform. These calls fell on deaf ears, and the Filipinos ultimately launched an armed revolution against Spain in 1896.

Above: **This painting is an artist's impression of how Magellan was killed by Lapu-Lapu in the first war between the Philippine natives and the Spanish in the sixteenth century.**

Left: **On February 15, 1898, the battleship USS *Maine* exploded and sank in Havana Harbor in Cuba. Although the cause of the explosion has never been fully determined, many Americans, at that time, blamed the Spanish military in Cuba for sinking the vessel. This event sparked the Spanish-American war.**

American Colony

The Philippines declared its independence from Spain on June 12, 1898, but the break from foreign rule was short-lived. In April 1898, the United States declared war on Spain, and battles between these two countries took place in both Cuba and the Philippines. The Filipinos fought alongside the Americans because they thought the United States would let them remain independent after the war. On December 10, 1898, to avoid formal defeat, Spain ceded the Philippines to the United States for U.S. $20 million under the Treaty of Paris. Upon approval by the U.S. Congress, the Philippines became a U.S. colony. The Filipinos tried to rebel against American rule, but their attempts were quashed by the U.S. military.

The Filipinos, however, did benefit from their new colonizer. Improvements were made in the areas of government and education. Unlike the Spaniards, who had refused to involve the Filipinos in public administration, U.S. officials trained them as civil servants, and a government similar to that of the United States was established in the process. Filipinos were also trained as schoolteachers for a new educational system that used English as a medium of instruction. Schools were open to all Filipinos.

UNIQUE PHILIPPINE TRANSPORTATION

In the Philippines, anyone can flag down a U.S. army jeep and tell the driver to go wherever he or she wants! This is because these jeeps (*below*) are no longer part of the military but part of a fleet of unique Philippine minibuses called jeepneys.
(*A Closer Look*, page 72)

Japanese Occupation and Independence

The bombing of Pearl Harbor in Hawaii on December 7, 1941, led the United States to declare war on Japan. As the Philippines was a U.S. colony located near Japan, the islands became a target for the Japanese military. After some fierce battles, the Americans lost the Philippines to Japan in May 1942. The U.S. army surrendered while under the command of General Jonathan M. Wainwright, and the Japanese occupied the Philippines from 1942 to 1945. They supposedly wanted to liberate the country from Western control, but Filipinos appointed by the Japanese authorities to form the Philippine government during that time were little more than puppets, and the Japanese remained firmly in control of the country. Throughout World War II, Japanese and American forces fought many naval, air, and land battles around the Philippines. The Japanese surrendered in 1945 and the Americans regained control of the Philippines. Over four centuries of foreign rule ended when the Republic of the Philippines was established on July 4, 1946.

Below: U.S. general Douglas MacArthur and some of his men wade ashore onto Leyte on October 20, 1944. MacArthur's mission was to free the Philippines from Japanese rule. On September 2, 1945, the Japanese surrendered.

Marcos and Martial Law

The Philippine people enjoyed democracy for twenty-six years before losing it again. On September 21, 1972, President Ferdinand Marcos declared martial law. Marcos replaced the elected legislature with a parliament that was loyal to him, establishing his reputation as a dictator. Marcos used the Philippine military to police the country, arresting those who opposed him on charges that they were communist agents. Instances of government corruption and human-rights violations peaked during his regime. The Marcos years ended with the bloodless People Power Revolution (also known as the EDSA revolution) in February 1986. Since then, Presidents Maria Corazon Aquino, Fidel V. Ramos, and Joseph E. Estrada have all striven to protect freedom and democracy in the Philippines.

Above: **Ferdinand Marcos and his wife, Imelda Marcos, were notorious for their extravagant lifestyle.**

PEOPLE POWER

The bloodless revolution is also known as the EDSA revolution of February 1986. EDSA stands for Epifanio De Los Santos Avenue, a major highway in Manila. This highway was where the pro-Marcos and anti-Marcos forces started a confrontation that ultimately led to the fall of Marcos.

Left: **This bust of Marcos, carved on the side of Mount Sto Tomas, stands along Marcos Highway, which leads into the city of Baguio.**

Maria Corazon Aquino (1933–)

Maria Corazon Aquino was the first woman president of the Republic of the Philippines. Her life took a dramatic turn when her husband, Benigno Aquino, was assassinated in August 1983. In a bid to continue his work as the chief political opponent of President Marcos, she went from being a homemaker to a politician overnight. In early February 1986, Aquino challenged Marcos in a snap presidential election. Although she won, Marcos refused to step down. Aquino then organized the bloodless People Power Revolution that ended the Marcos regime in late February. During her term, Aquino implemented much-needed social and economic reforms.

Maria Corazon Aquino

Fidel Valdez Ramos (1928–)

Fidel Valdez Ramos was, along with Corazon Aquino, a major driving force behind the EDSA revolution. A career soldier, General Ramos graduated from the U.S. Military Academy at West Point, N.Y. While he was reputedly a close associate of former president Ferdinand Marcos, Ramos, who was then the vice chief of staff of the Armed Forces of the Philippines (AFP), joined Aquino in her fight against Marcos. When Aquino became president, she promoted him to chief of staff. In 1988, he became the country's defense minister. In 1992, Ramos ran for president and won. The country's economy improved dramatically while he was in office.

Fidel Valdez Ramos

Joseph Ejercito Estrada (1937–)

Joseph Ejercito Estrada, like former U.S. president Ronald Reagan, was an actor before he became president. As an actor, Estrada was the first person in Philippine cinematic history to have won five FAMAS awards (the Philippine equivalent of the Academy Award) for Best Actor, the last of which he won in 1981. Estrada's political career began in 1968 when he ran for mayor of San Juan, a city in Metro Manila. He remained mayor there for sixteen years, and the city flourished under his leadership. Over the years, Estrada won awards for being one of "Ten Outstanding Young Men in Public Administration," an "Outstanding Mayor," and a "Foremost Nationalist." In 1998, Estrada became the country's thirteenth president.

Joseph Ejercito Estrada

Government and the Economy

Promises of Democracy

After the fall of Marcos in 1986, a new constitution was enacted in the following year. As a result of the 1987 Constitution, the Philippines resumed a presidential form of government. The elected president, however, can serve only one six-year term, and he or she is assisted by an elected vice president and an appointed cabinet. Malacañang Palace in Manila is the Philippine president's official residence and office.

Below: **The Philippine president lives and works in Malacañang Palace, which is situated along the Pasig River in Manila.**

In 1987, the Philippine Congress was also elected, replacing the questionable parliament that Marcos established during his dictatorship. Under the 1987 Constitution, the president can neither dissolve Congress nor declare martial law without the review and support of Congress. In keeping with the American system it was modeled after, the Philippine Congress has two houses — the Senate, or the Upper House, which consists of twenty-four senators, and the House of Representatives, or the Lower House, which has a maximum of 250 members. A senator serves a maximum of two six-year terms, while a representative serves a maximum of three three-year terms.

Local Government and the Armed Forces

Under the 1991 Local Government Code (Republic Act 7160), many administrative responsibilities previously handled by the national government were passed on to local government units, or LGUs. The different categories of LGUs are provinces, cities, municipalities, and *barangays* (bar-RUNG-guys), or village communities. LGUs help establish various organizations, such as school and health boards, that are aimed at improving the overall standard of living in their respective localities. LGUs are also at liberty to impose local taxes or provide monetary incentives for people. LGUs foster a strong sense of community among their residents by encouraging them to participate in public meetings and projects.

CONSTITUTIONS OF 1935, 1973, AND 1987

Implemented when the Philippines was still a U.S. colony, the 1935 Constitution gave Filipinos unprecedented control over domestic governmental affairs. The 1973 Constitution established Marcos' dictatorial powers. A democratic constitution was passed in 1987 under President Aquino.

While most countries have three branches of government — legislative, judicial, and executive — some political analysts say the Philippines has four because the Armed Forces of the Philippines (AFP) greatly influences the decisions of the Philippine government. In times of peace, the AFP aids rural development programs, helping civilians build roads, schools, and playgrounds. The AFP also provides assistance when disasters happen. Although highly trained, the AFP has rather dated equipment. This situation, however, is improving with the AFP modernization plan passed in July 1994. The plan allows the AFP to buy better weapons, naval vessels, and tactical aircraft.

Above: **Many Philippine government buildings were designed to resemble government buildings in the United States. Shown above is the Philippine Congress Building in Manila.**

Untouched Natural Resources

The Philippines is blessed with many natural resources, a large proportion of which remains unexploited. The country is rich in forests and marine life, as well as in mineral and energy sources. Philippine marine life, for example, ranges from one of the world's largest fish, the huge whale shark (*Rhincodon typus*), to one of the world's smallest fish, the dwarf pygmy (*Pandaka pygmaea*). Other marine products, such as mollusks, seaweed, shellfish, sponges, and pearls, are plentiful. Pearl oysters, in particular, are abundant around the Sulu Archipelago.

Mineral resources, including nickel, copper, iron, and gold, are also abundant. Gold mining is common in Mountain province on the island of Luzon, as well as on Masbate and Mindanao. The oldest and by far the best copper mine in the Philippines still operates in the Mountain province. Iron and nickel deposits are concentrated in Surigao del Norte, a province on the northern tip of Mindanao. Marble deposits are found on the islands of Mindoro, Romblon, and Palawan. The Philippines is also endowed with large reserves of geothermal energy and natural gas, which, if developed fully, would provide the country with all its energy needs.

Above: **Trawlers drop off their catch at Manila Harbor fish port. Fish are rinsed and sorted before they are sold.**

Below: **Philippine pearls are among the largest in the world.**

Agriculture and Industry

The economy of the Philippines relies heavily on agriculture. Almost 40 percent of the workforce is involved in this sector. Local plantations yield crops such as rice, corn, sweet potatoes, sugar, fruits, and tobacco. The Philippines is the world's biggest producer of coconuts and hemp products. The country ranks second for sugar production and fifth for tobacco. Philippine fruits, such as mangoes, pineapples, oranges, papayas, and bananas, are exported globally. Dole, a major American food company, grows and cans pineapples on the island of Mindanao. Philippine bananas are stocked in supermarkets all over Asia.

The manufacturing sector of the Philippines has been expanding rapidly since the 1950s, focusing especially on processed food, cloth, medicine, chemicals, wood products, and oil refining. The Philippines generally imports more than it exports. Leading imports are petroleum, heavy machinery, and metal ores, as well as electrical and electronic goods. Among its trading partners, Japan and the United States are the most prominent. The Philippines also trades with many neighboring Asian countries.

Below: **A woman checks on the harvest at Larpanday Banana Plantation, near the city of Davao on the island of Mindanao.**

People and Lifestyle

Ethnicity

The majority of Filipinos today are descendants of Philippine natives, or Negritos, and early Malay migrants who came from Malaysia and Indonesia. Filipinos of Malay ancestry account for 95.5 percent of the population, while 1.5 percent are Chinese. The remaining 3 percent are of other races or ethnicities.

The Visayans, the Tagalogs, and the Ilocanos are major ethnic groups in the Philippines. While the Visayans live on the country's central islands, the Tagalogs and the Ilocanos both reside on Luzon. Apart from these three groups, about 1.6 million Filipinos belong to a variety of ethnic minorities. More than half of these are Muslims who reside on the western part of Mindanao and also on parts of the Sulu Archipelago. Other ethnic minorities tend to live in the mountains of Cordillera Central. Almost four centuries of Spanish rule and extensive trade with Chinese merchants dating back to the ninth century have given rise to another ethnic group — *mestizos* (mis-TEE-sohs), or people of mixed Spanish or Chinese and Filipino ancestry.

BANAUE RICE TERRACES

The Banaue rice terraces were built by the Ifugao tribe some 3,000 years ago. The Ifugaos were headhunters before they turned to rice cultivation.
(A Closer Look, page 46)

Below: These women are from the Ifugao tribe, an ethnic minority in the Philippines. They live in Cordillera Central, in the northern Philippines.

Left: Decked with Christmas decorations, this modern shopping center on Cebu is where wealthy Filipinos shop.

The Philippines, like many of its neighboring Asian countries, has a huge disparity between the rich and the poor. Dividing the Philippine population into three categories — the rich, the middle class, and the poor — puts this disparity in perspective. The rich make up about 15 percent of the Philippine population, and they command about 85 percent of the country's wealth. They are mostly landowners or members of wealthy families who control major businesses in the Philippines. These families are usually mestizos.

The middle class consists of about 20 percent of the population. Middle-class Filipinos are mostly successful professionals, such as doctors, lawyers, bankers, engineers, and architects.

The poor account for a staggering 65 percent of the population, and they possess only 10 percent of the country's wealth. Some people in this category lack even the basic necessities, and over 30 percent of Filipinos live below the poverty line. Many Filipinos have migrated overseas in search of better economic prospects.

AN ETHNIC MINORITY

Only 5 percent of Filipinos are Muslim. Most of them live on or near Mindanao in the southern Philippines.
(*A Closer Look, page 54*)

Above: **This young Filipino couple has just exchanged vows in a cathedral in Manila.**

Family Ties

Filipinos have unusually tight-knit families, and they count on their families, and even their extended families, for help when faced with problems of any kind. Many Filipinos actually live with their extended families, and those families that do not live together meet with their relatives on a regular basis. Gathering only on special occasions or public holidays is simply not enough for Filipinos.

The influence of Roman Catholicism in the Philippines has led Filipinos to regard children as a blessing from God, rendering them intense sources of pride and joy. Although spurred by good intentions, Philippine parents sometimes interfere in their children's affairs, even after their children become adults. Some Philippine parents go so far as to influence their children's choice of a job or spouse. Philippine children, on the other hand, are expected to be obedient and loyal to their parents for as long as they live. Regardless of the circumstances, a Filipino must never talk back to his or her parents as it is considered despicable and infinitely disrespectful.

TRADITIONAL GAMES CHILDREN PLAY

Traditional Philippine games are so enjoyable and so inexpensive that they are still popular with children today.

(*A Closer Look, page 70*)

Values, Culture, and Tradition

Philippine society is characterized by a number of positive attributes, such as a respect for authority, a resilient attitude, and a high regard for *amor propio* (ah-MOOR pro-PEE-oh), or the extreme care people take to maintain their own and other people's dignities. Filipinos also have *bayanihan* (BAH-YAH-nee-hun), or a sense of community, and believe strongly in *utang na loob* (oo-TUNG nah loh-OHB), or repaying favors with gratitude.

On a less positive note, Filipinos can be somewhat fatalistic and may practice *mañana* (MUN-yah-nah), or procrastination, purely out of habit. They may also show poor sportsmanship, or *pikon* (PEE-con). Some Filipinos are guilty of *ningas kogon* (NING-us koh-GONE), which means that they are always enthusiastic about starting new projects but do not always finish them.

The Filipinos' respect for authority is an extension of the traditional respect given to older family members. This attitude tends to compromise independent thinking and gives those in authority a great deal of power. In day-to-day living, the Filipinos value high standards of neatness and cleanliness, not only in their personal grooming but also in their homes.

Below: **Spending a leisurely Sunday together, this Filipino family stops for some drinks and snacks in Rizal Park, Manila.**

Education

Basic education in the Philippines consists of six years of elementary school and four years of high school. Children enter elementary school at the age of seven and are taught in both Pilipino and English. Before the nation gained independence in 1946, all classes were taught in English. Since then, Pilipino has been increasingly emphasized, and both languages are official languages. Until 1987, the study of Spanish was compulsory, and students in high school and college had to contend with three languages — Pilipino, English, and Spanish. Today, optional languages in the school curriculum include Mandarin Chinese and other regional languages or dialects. The Philippine Department of Education, Culture, and Sports supervises both public and private schools.

At 94 percent, the Philippines has the third-highest literacy rate in Asia, after Japan and South Korea, respectively. Approximately nine out of ten Filipinos aged ten and above can write and understand a simple message in at least one language or dialect. Within the Philippines, the Metro Manila region has the highest literacy rate at 98.8 percent, while the autonomous region of Muslim Mindanao has the lowest literacy rate at 73.5 percent.

Below: **These children are attending a public school in the city of Davao on Mindanao.**

Above: **Statues of nine Philippine martyr-saints stand in front of the library of the University of Santo Tomas in Manila.**

The high literacy rate in the Philippines can be attributed to two major factors: first, Filipinos regard educating their children as gravely important; and second, elementary education for children between ages seven and twelve is compulsory and free.

Schools in the Philippines are either government or private institutions, and the disparity in the tuition fees is remarkable. Private schools are costly, making them inaccessible to most Philippine students. Figures show that 93 percent of elementary school students and 69 percent of high school students are enrolled in government schools. Private universities are usually run by religious groups, thus their school curricula are slightly different from those of public universities. Religion and theology, for instance, are taught only in private universities.

Founded by Spanish Dominican priests in 1611, the University of Santo Tomas is the oldest university in the Philippines. In 1927, the university moved from Intramuros, an area in Manila enclosed by high walls, to where it is today in the district of Sampaloc in Manila. Since it was founded, the university stopped operating only twice — when the Philippines revolted against the U.S. (1898–1899) and when the Japanese occupied Manila (1942–1945).

HISTORIC CITY OF MANILA

In the sixteenth century, the Spanish built walls around a large section of Manila, the capital of the Philippines, to protect themselves from being invaded by Muslims and other foreigners. The name of this city within a city is Intramuros.
(A Closer Look, page 58)

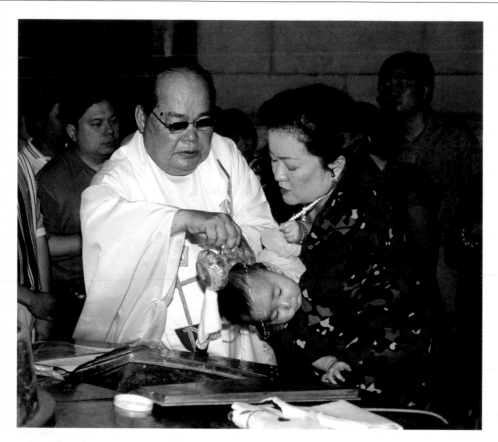

Left: **This baby is one of many babies baptized in the Philippines each day. Eighty-three percent of Filipinos are Catholic.**

Religion

Except for the Muslims from the island of Mindanao and the Sulu Archipelago, early Filipinos were animistic pagans who worshiped ancestral spirits called *anitos* (ah-NEE-tohs), which they believed resided in rivers, mountains, old trees, and fields. The Philippines converted to Christianity when the Spaniards arrived. At present, 83 percent of Filipinos are Roman Catholics, 9 percent are Protestants, and 5 percent are Muslims. The remaining 3 percent of Filipinos are either Buddhists or members of other religious minorities.

Religion plays an important role in the everyday lives of modern Filipinos. Houses, cars, and offices are often blessed by a priest before they are used. Philippine parents regard their children's baptisms as special occasions. Filipinos also have a tradition of attending Mass on their birthdays. Some pagan ceremonies are still practiced in the Philippines, but they have a Christian twist. When clearing a plot of land for planting, for instance, a shaman sprinkles a cross with rice wine and inspects the flight patterns and entrails of birds for encoded omens.

Superstitions and Other Beliefs

Early Filipinos believed in the magical power of sorcerers and witchcraft, and this pagan culture continues to figure prominently in the lives of Filipinos today.

Filipinos believe in *multo* (mool-TOH) and *mangkukulam* (MUNG-koo-koo-lum), ghosts and witches, respectively. These figures can assume the form of any animal. Filipinos also subscribe to *kulam* (KOO-lum), which, like voodoo, is a belief that people can be harmed when a toy or an effigy of them is pricked with needles. Filipinos believe amulets or charms, such as the *anting-anting* (UN-ting-UN-ting), possess magical powers that make them invincible against iron weapons. The *gayuma* (gah-YOO-mah) is a love potion that is used to evoke the affection of a woman. A magical herb called *odom* (OH-dohm) is believed to make its possessor invisible to the human eye, while the *uiga* (oo-WEE-gah), a Visayan charm, supposedly prevents its owner from becoming wet when he or she swims across rivers.

In a culture rich in myths and folklore, it is not surprising that Philippine children's literature also is filled with fascinating mythical creatures and other personalities.

Below: **Quiapo mosque is one of the places where Muslims in Manila go to pray.**

27

Language and Literature

A Multilingual People and Their Literature

More than one hundred dialects or native languages are spoken throughout the Philippines, and they all belong to the family of Malayo-Polynesian languages. Both English and Pilipino are official languages in the Philippines. Pilipino was derived from Tagalog, one of the eight main native languages of the country. The remaining seven are Cebuano, Ilocano, Ilonggo, Bicolano, Waray-waray, Kapampangan, and Pangasinan.

Ancient Philippine literature comes in both oral and written forms. Very little written literature, however, survived the Spanish Conquest. Oral literature, on the other hand, was preserved by word of mouth. Folklore and epics that celebrate the deeds of gods and heroes passed from one generation to the next in a variety of Philippine languages and dialects. Some famous epics include *Hudhud and Alim* from the Ifugao tribe and *Biag ni Lam-ang* from the Ilocanos. The "Prince of Filipino Poets," Francisco Baltazar, earned a living by penning *awits* (er-WITS), *moro-moro* (MOH-roh-MOH-roh), and other forms of native poetry.

Left: **This newspaper vendor in Manila holds up one of the many publications he has for sale. In the Philippines, local newspapers, periodicals, and books come in a wide variety of languages, including English and some of the native languages.**

Dr. José P. Rizal (1861–1896) Hero and Literary Genius

Born in the district of Calamba in the Laguna province, Dr. José P. Rizal is the national hero of the Philippines and is revered throughout Southeast Asia as a Malay hero and martyr. His prolific writings evoked patriotism among the Filipinos. For Rizal, the excesses of the Spanish were the main cause of his country's political and economic woes. This view was reflected in two of his better-known novels, *Noli Me Tangere*, or *Touch Me Not*, and its sequel *El Filibusterismo*, or *The Reign of Greed*. In 1892, Rizal founded *La Liga Filipina*, an organization that advocated political reform in the country. In August 1896, he was tried by a Spanish military court for assisting in the rebellion against Spain. Rizal was executed by firing squad in Manila on December 30, 1896.

Above: Noli Me Tangere, one of Rizal's two most influential novels, heavily criticizes the Spanish colonizers.

Arts

Theater

One of the oldest forms of Philippine theater is moro-moro, a literary genre of plays in verse that portray the conflict between the Christians and the Muslims, or Moros. The construction of the first Philippine theaters in the nineteenth century led to the increased popularity of zarzuela, or satirical opera. The Spaniards often used moro-moro as a vehicle for their propaganda, while patriotic Filipinos used zarzuela to counter pro-Spanish sentiments, voicing their social and political criticism through the operas.

Although the popularity of stage performances waned with the onset of movie theaters early in the twentieth century, some theater companies have sought, in recent years, to revive these traditional theatrical forms. Lea Salonga, Philippine singer and stage performer, made Filipinos proud when she won both the Tony and the Laurence Olivier awards in 1991 for her outstanding work as Kim, the lead in *Miss Saigon*, on Broadway and London's West End, respectively.

FAMOUS FILIPINO PAINTERS

Juan Luna and Felix Hidalgo were among the first Philippine artists to gain international recognition. Several of their works have won art competitions in Europe.
(*A Closer Look, page 56*)

Below: Bayanihan dancers perform traditional Philippine dance theater outside the Malacañang Palace in Manila.

Above: The Spanish left a legacy of Baroque architecture in many parts of the country.

Architecture

In its pre-Spanish days, houses in the Philippines were made of nipa, bamboo, and various native woods. Early versions of these houses were made without using nails or pegs. To facilitate ventilation, these houses, called *bahay kubo* (BAH-hay koo-BOH), were elevated 10 to 16 feet (3 to 5 m) off the ground, and their rooftops were pitched steeply.

When the Spanish arrived, they brought the Baroque style of architecture from Europe. This style can be seen in many churches still standing in the Philippines today. Spanish colonial architecture was an ingenious combination of Philippine, Spanish, and Mexican designs. Between the sixteenth and nineteenth centuries, the Baroque style was pervasive and was reflected in intricate grilles, wooden lattices, and ornate floor and wall tiles.

By the nineteenth century, however, a new style of domestic architecture, the Antillean house, emerged. These houses originated in Spanish colonies in the Antilles islands in the West Indies, including Cuba and Puerto Rico. Such houses were made entirely out of wood and had better ventilation.

BAHAY KUBO

The bahay kubo, or nipa hut, looks simple but shows great ingenuity in its design. This kind of hut is built with the understanding that a person's home should blend with its natural surroundings.
(A Closer Look, page 44)

31

Dance and Music

While Philippine folk dances may show hints of Malay, Muslim, and Spanish influences, these dances are, nevertheless, unique to Filipinos. The Jota Butanguena Polkabal, for instance, was always performed by the Spanish at social gatherings. Filipinos, however, have since adapted the dance and developed several variations, such as La Jota Moncadena and La Jota Manilena. The former is a combination of Spanish and Ilocano dance steps, accompanied by bamboo castanets, and the latter is Manila's version of the same dance.

Ethnic music in the Philippines has been influenced more by the country's own native communities than by the Spanish. Typical musical instruments include the *kudyapi* (kood-JAH-pee), which is a two-stringed instrument that resembles a lute, and the *git-git* (GEET-geet), which is a fiddle that has human hair for strings. The kudyapi originated with the Tiboli tribe of northern Mindanao, and the Mangyans and Negritos invented the git-git. The influence of native music has been so strong that music such as the *kundiman* (koon-DEE-mun), a simple ballad, still inspires songwriters today.

Above: **This Filipino performer sings at a pub in Manila. Singing and dancing are major parts of Philippine culture.**

Crafts

Every region of the Philippines specializes in a type of handicraft, such as basketry, brassware, or handwoven textiles. Some of the more popular handwoven textiles, such as *pina* (PEEN-yah), *jusi* (WHO-see), and *ramie* (RAH-mee), are used to make the *barong tagalog* (BAH-rong tah-GAH-lawg), the national costume of Filipino men. While pina is a delicate fabric that is woven from pineapple fibers, jusi, or "banana silk," is woven from raw silk threads. Ramie is similar to linen but is woven from grass fibers.

Beautiful brass items, such as trays, teapots, urns, jugs, and jewelry boxes, are produced on Mindanao. The small town of Paete, on the eastern shore of Laguna de Bay, is known for high-quality woodcarving, specializing in figurines, chess pieces, and plates. Basketwork from different parts of the Philippines bears distinctive designs. Baskets from Mindanao, for example, are distinguished by the black nito vine craftworkers used to produce a checkered pattern. The Ifugaos of northern Luzon, on the other hand, prefer smoke-stained materials for their basketry.

NATIONAL ATTIRE

A combination of creativity and imperial oppression brought about the national costume of the Philippines.
(A Closer Look, page 64)

Below: **A woman from Iloilo, on Panay, embroiders intricate designs on pina.**

Leisure and Festivals

Endless Festivity

Filipinos love fiestas. At least one fiesta is held nearly every month somewhere in the Philippines. Under Spanish rule, the Philippines celebrated many Catholic festivals, a move made by the Spaniards to encourage conversions to Catholicism. Today, these traditional Catholic festivals possess a distinctly Philippine style because they have been integrated with local beliefs and practices. Elaborate fireworks and street parades make these fiestas a kaleidoscope of colors. In recent years, beauty pageants have become part of Philippine fiestas, as well.

Leisure

The average Philippine family loves to window-shop, and many families spend their weekends together at various shopping malls. Open-air bazaars or flea markets are also popular with the Filipinos because they enjoy looking at the native handicrafts that

MAY: MONTH OF FESTIVALS

Filipinos love the month of May. Three of their favorite festivals are celebrated one after the other in this month.
(*A Closer Look,* page 62)

Below: **Filipinos in Manila are often treated to free concerts in Rizal Park on weekends.**

cannot be found in shopping centers. These handmade products often employ materials such as hemp, shells, wood, and pineapple fibers.

Filipinos also love watching television or going to the movies. Ratings show that they favor miniseries or soap operas from the United States. The Philippines, however, does not import all its audiovisual entertainment. The country produces many of its own films and television programs, contributing to a diverse selection on both the big and small screens. With modern technology, an even larger variety of programs is available to Philippine viewers if they subscribe to cable or paid television networks. As not all households can afford a television set, it is not uncommon for children and adults alike to sit on stools outside their neighbors' homes and watch programs from their neighbors' television sets.

Another pastime favored by the Filipinos is good conversation. In fact, the Filipinos are particularly fond of engaging in impassioned discussions about politics. On the lighter side, they also love to talk about the lives of local actors and actresses.

Above: **Billboards advertising both local and imported movies, such as these in the city of Davao, can be found everywhere in the Philippines.**

Above: **Villagers watch as these young Filipinos play a game of basketball.**

Sports

Despite being small in stature, Filipinos are very fond of basketball. This passion for basketball is a legacy of the country's American colonizers. The Philippine Basketball Association (PBA) is one of the oldest professional sports leagues in Asia. Amateur and professional basketball competitions are played all year round in almost every part of the country. At least one basketball court can be found in nearly every village in the Philippines.

While the Philippines has not produced basketball players who can compete with their taller American or European counterparts, the country has produced world-class boxers, bowlers, golfers, martial artists, and billiard players. Six-time world champion Paeng Nepomuceno, for example, has won four Bowling World Cups, in 1976, 1980, 1992, and 1996. He also won the International Tournament held in Las Vegas, Nevada, in 1984 and the 1999 World Tenpin Masters held in London, England. A 7-foot (2.1-m) tall tribute to this great Filipino athlete stands at the International Bowling Hall of Fame in St. Louis, Missouri. The man himself is 6 feet 2 inches (1.88 m) tall.

SABONG: KING OF SPORTS

Many Filipinos find themselves unable to turn away from a round of *sabong* **(SAH-bong), or cockfighting.**
(A Closer Look, page 68)

Sabong, or cockfighting, and jai alai are two popular spectator sports in the Philippines. The latter originated in the Basque region of Spain and is a version of Spanish handball. Jai alai is similar to squash, in that it is also played on a court enclosed by high walls. Instead of a racket, however, each player uses a crescent-shaped wicker basket called a cesta, which looks like an extension of the arm, to catch an oncoming ball or to whisk it against the wall, sometimes at speeds exceeding 150 miles per hour (240 km per hour)!

Another spectator sport is *sipa* (SEE-pah), which means "kick." True to its name, sipa involves constantly kicking a hollow rattan (cane) ball into the air to prevent it from touching the ground. Players can use only their knees, legs, and feet. The sport, which is played on a rectangular court divided by a high net, can be played one-on-one, in doubles, or in teams of four.

Contestants of a traditional fiesta sport, *palo sebo* (PAH-loh SEE-boh), climb a heavily greased bamboo pole in an attempt to get to the top, where a cash prize sits. It is difficult to get to the top, but some contestants make it easier on themselves by covering their bodies with ash to get a better grip on the pole.

Above: **Players of jai alai must have both agility and stamina.**

Below: **A crowd gathers to watch this amateur boxing match on Mindanao.**

Religious Festivals

As Filipinos are predominantly Roman Catholic, the Lenten season and Christmas are the most widely celebrated holidays in the Philippines. The Lenten season, or Holy Week, consists of the days preceding the crucifixion of Jesus Christ. The days are characterized throughout the nation by a mood so solemn that everything slows to a virtual stop. Television programs, for example, are limited, and those aired are normally religious in nature. Some older Filipinos go as far as to forbid listening to loud music during this time of year.

To mark Holy Week, many Filipinos practice penance. While some Filipinos reenact the death of Jesus in dramatizations, others play the role of Christ by actually performing the crucifixion. These Filipinos have their palms nailed to a cross either as punishment for their sins or as a display of their faith. Another type of penance involves skinning one's knees on rough church floors. On Good Friday, some Filipinos actually pay others to strike their bare backs with rope lashes. Filipinos who practice penance, however, do it as a voluntary act of faith.

Above: **Public crucifixions are commonly seen in the Philippines during Holy Week. These extreme acts are performed by Filipinos who wish to atone for their sins.**

PHILIPPINE CHURCHES

Some of the grandest Philippine churches were built during the time of Spanish colonization.

(A Closer Look, page 66)

Ati-Atihan

The *Ati-Atihan* (ah-TEE-AH-tee-hun) in Kalibo is an annual three-day event held in the third week of January. Kalibo is the city center of the Aklan province on the island of Panay. The festival commemorates the arrival of four Bornean *datus* (DAH-toos), or chiefs, in 1212. These datus purchased Panay from King Marikduo of the Aetas, a community of pygmy-like aborigines, for a headdress, a necklace, and a basin. To celebrate their acquisition and newfound friendship, the datus organized a feast for the natives and blackened their own faces with soot to better resemble their new friends.

Today, many revelers blacken their faces with soot and dress like the thirteenth-century aborigines to mark the occasion. The different Ati tribes that live on separate parts of Panay, however, distinguish themselves by wearing specific colors or coded patterns. For three days, revelers make their way to the lavishly decorated town square in ritualized dances. The Ati-Atihan includes a holy Mass on the last day, a Sunday, in the local Church of Santo Niño. This Mass is followed by a four-hour procession of the tribes and their gaily decorated floats.

CORDILLERA PEOPLE

Many tribes reside in and around Cordillera Central, a mountainous region in the northern Philippines.
(A Closer Look, page 48)

Left: **These girls are wearing tribal costumes that are unique to their community, to celebrate Ati-Atihan.**

Food

Good Food and Manners

Nearly all Filipinos eat rice every day. In fact, some eat it three times a day — for breakfast, lunch, and dinner. A typical Filipino meal includes rice, meat or fish, and vegetables. As Filipinos have a mixture of Malay, Spanish, and Chinese ancestry, Philippine cuisine is similarly eclectic, with hints of American, Arab, and Indian influences as well. It is also customary for Filipinos to snack twice a day, once midmorning and once midafternoon.

Filipinos have generally retained the tradition of eating with their fingers. Many modern Philippine families, however, prefer to use cutlery. When Filipinos are eating, they are expected to invite the people around them to share the meal, especially if they have visitors arrive at their homes during mealtimes. Hosts are considered very impolite if they do not ask visitors to join them at the dinner table. Also, in Philippine culture, dinner is the most important meal of the day. Family members who are away during the day make it a point to gather for dinner.

Below: **Filipinos enjoy eating heartily, and everyone is welcome to join in.**

Above: **This food stall, inside one of Manila's modern shopping centers, sells traditional local dishes.**

Traditional Filipino Dishes

Traditional Philippine appetizers include *chicharon* (TSEE-tsah-rone) and *kinilaw* (kee-nee-LAW), which are pork crackling and marinated raw fish, respectively. These appetizers are also generally referred to as *pulutan* (poo-loo-TUN). *Adobo* (AH-doh-boh) is sometimes called the national dish, and it can be either pork or chicken marinated in vinegar, soy sauce, garlic, and spices. In most cases, a feast in the Philippines would not be complete without a *lechon* (LEHR-tsone), or suckling pig, which is stuffed with various spices and roasted until the skin is crispy and the meat tender. A Philippine dish is also never complete without an accompanying sauce. A simple, everyday sauce is made out of vinegar, hot chilli or soy sauce, and lime juice.

The most popular dessert in the Philippines is *halo-halo* (HAH-loh-HAH-loh), which literally means "mixed." Local fruits, such as jackfruit and coconut, are mixed with crushed ice. The mixture is served with a scoop of ice cream and some milk. Philippine ice cream includes flavors such as yam and coconut.

DELICIOUS LECHON

Filipinos usually have lechon, or roasted suckling pig, when they throw big parties. It takes a lot of work and patience to make this dish.
(A Closer Look, page 50)

A CLOSER LOOK AT THE PHILIPPINES

Experts believe the first people to migrate to the Philippines arrived about forty thousand years ago. They were the ancestors of the Philippine natives called Negritos or Aeta today. The Philippine character has since been influenced by several cultures, including aborigine, Indian, Chinese, Spanish, and American. The capital city of Manila, with its Spanish-style churches and its American-style government buildings, embodies this rich cultural history. Religion is a powerful influence in the Philippines, but Filipinos also love such secular pastimes as gambling on cockfights. Among the natural treasures of the Philippines are breathtaking rice terraces, volcanoes, and beaches. The nation is, however, facing the possible extinction of some of its wildlife, such as the Philippine eagle and the dugong.

Opposite: **Built by the Ifugao tribe over three thousand years ago, the Banaue rice terraces are an awesome sight.**

Below: **Native Filipinos today are of mixed descent. Aborigine, Malay, Indonesian, and Negrito cultures all influence the Philippine heritage.**

Bahay Kubo

The bahay kubo, or nipa hut, is to a Filipino what an igloo is to an Inuit of the Arctic. This traditional Filipino home is simple yet functional. It is usually raised about 10 to 16 feet (3 to 5 m) off the ground by four or more posts made of either bamboo or wood. Elevating the hut from the ground improves air circulation both inside and outside the hut. It also protects the occupants from floods, which is important because most bahay kubo settlements are near rivers or the sea. Creating distance from the ground also deters mice and bugs from entering the hut. As for the occupants, they climb in and out using a ladder that can be drawn up at night.

The space underneath the bahay kubo is called the *silong* (SEE-long). It is often used as a storage area, a granary, or a pen for ducks and chickens. Cooking is done outside the hut, on the ground below. Jars of water are also kept outside for washing purposes.

Below: **Members of this Filipino family living in this bahay kubo on Boracay Island are doing their daily chores.**

Left: This boy from Mindoro stares out the window of his nipa hut. The cover of leaves propped up above the window is secured over it at night.

The bahay kubo usually has only four walls, enclosing a simple, multipurpose space. Most bahay kubos also have windows. Larger huts have partitions, while other huts may have rooms. The walls can be made of nipa, dried grass, or wood. The floor is made by slatting halved bamboo stems with the shiny curved sides facing up, inside the hut. The curved surfaces actually help keep the hut clean because dirt slips easily between the gaps and falls right through the floor. These gaps also improve ventilation inside the hut.

To shade its occupants from the sun, the bahay kubo usually has a roof of nipa shingle or thatch made of cogon, a coarse grass. Its window coverings, too, are made of such materials. They are propped open during the day and tightly secured at night.

Building the bahay kubo is a communal activity. Filipinos putting together a new hut are always assisted by their relatives and future neighbors. When the hut is completed, it is customary for the occupants to throw a big party, providing food and drinks for everyone who helped. The parish priest is invited afterward to bless the new home and its occupants.

Banaue Rice Terraces

Located on Luzon, about 31 miles (50 km) southeast of Bontoc, the rice terraces of Banaue are sometimes referred to as the "Eighth Wonder of the World." They are believed to be over three thousand years old. The rice terraces are just over 100 square miles (260 square km) in area and peak at approximately 4,000 feet (1,220 m) above sea level.

The Ifugaos, who were once a tribe of headhunters, used crude hand tools to build these terraces. They also reinforced

the entire base of the mountains with stones to prevent erosion. Although the paddies were carved out of hard soil, keeping water seepage at a minimum, an irrigation system was still developed as a precautionary measure. The entire community came together to build it, and, to this day, the community maintains it.

The weight of the stones moved by the tribe to build as well as maintain these terraces during the three thousand years is believed to surpass the weight of the stones used to build the ancient pyramids of Egypt. These terraces are also strategically angled to receive ample sunlight.

Above: **The Banaue rice terraces are on the island of Luzon in the northern Philippines.**

The Ifugaos are self-sufficient as a community. They neither travel extensively in search of food nor depend on hunting for survival. Thus, they have managed to remain largely untouched by outside influences.

In an abiding tradition of gender roles, women today still perform the actual planting, while men maintain the rice paddies, the stone walls, and the irrigation system. Men are also responsible for harvesting the grain.

Different levels of wealth also exists within the Ifugao society. The rich own the lower and larger terraces, while the less privileged own the higher and narrower terraces.

Below: **In keeping with the tribe's gender roles, these Ifugao women are planting rice.**

The terraces, which require constant care, are currently under threat because many young Ifugaos are migrating to nearby towns and cities to seek employment, instead of working in the paddy fields. If this trend persists, the terraces will be left untilled and will eventually dry out and waste away. Another problem facing the terraces is land erosion caused by the illegal logging of surrounding forests. To protect the terraces, the Philippine government has declared the Banaue rice terraces a National Park Reserve. The rice terraces are also recognized by the United Nations Educational, Scientific, and Cultural Organization (UNESCO) as "a living cultural landscape."

Cordillera People

The Benguets, Bontocs, Apayaos, Kalingas, and Ifugaos are the five major ethnic minorities residing in Cordillera Central. Collectively, they are called Igorots, which means "people from the mountains." These mountain folk live sedentary lives based on agriculture and maintain age-old customs of worshiping tribal spirits and ancestors.

The Benguets live in the province of Benguet in the southern part of Cordillera Central. They grow rice, coffee, and vegetables and raise livestock. The Benguets often take their produce to the marketplace in Baguio, a place many Filipinos visit in summer to

Left: **Apart from rice cultivation, woodcarving is a large part of Ifugao culture. This man is carving a duck.**

Above: **This woman is weaving cloth as her child watches. They live in a remote area near Banaue.**

enjoy the cooler climate. At community feasts, where ritualized animal sacrifice is the focal activity, the Benguets distinguish themselves by donning ceremonial blankets.

The Bontocs live in the province of Mountain. Early Bontocs were extremely receptive to American missionary teaching, which explains why they prefer to speak English instead of their native language today. Apart from making pottery and wooden figurines, they also mine gold and copper. The Bontocs hang coffins in cliffs and caves, an ancient burial practice unique to their tribe.

The Apayaos live along the western edge of the province of Kalinga-Apayao. Unlike the Bontocs, American missionaries had little influence on the Apayaos. They are animistic and very traditional, and they still use bows and arrows to hunt. The Apayaos also enjoy fast music and dancing and have a tradition of body tattoos.

The Kalingas live in other areas of Kalinga-Apayao. Like the Ifugaos, who built the Banaue rice terraces, they were once a tribe of headhunters. Headhunting was central to the lives of the Kalingas, who treated it as a measure of male prestige. They stopped headhunting only about two generations ago. Today, dignity and hospitality are two qualities heavily emphasized in their culture.

Delicious Lechon

For most Filipinos, a grand feast is not complete without lechon, or roasted pig. Lechon, derived from the Spanish word *leche*, meaning "milk," is almost always the centerpiece of parties. In keeping with its name, a suckling pig, a pig that still feeds on its mother's milk, is preferred when preparing lechon because its flesh stays tender while its skin becomes crispy.

To make good lechon, the pig must be cleaned well, with all its entrails removed and its skin scrubbed. The cavity of the pig's body is then stuffed with different spices before being skewered lengthwise with a spit, from its mouth to its backside. Finally, the pig is rotated over hot coals for four hours.

The technique of roasting the pig is crucial; within this technique lies the secret to good lechon. First, hot coals are arranged in two heaps, one on either side of the pig. These coals are placed about 3 feet (0.9 m) away from the pig so that the pig cooks slowly, allowing the meat of the pig to cook before the skin burns. As it roasts, the piled coals gradually are moved closer to the pig. In the meantime, the pig's skin is brushed with salt and water. When the skin is crisp, lard is applied as a final touch.

Left: **An ice cream vendor in Manila parks his stall in front of a row of freshly roasted lechon. Filipinos love lechon so much that some restaurants have begun to make it daily so that Filipinos can indulge in their favorite dish without having to wait for a special occasion.**

50

Different regions of the Philippines use different ingredients to flavor the meat. On Cebu, the cleaned, empty belly of the pig is stuffed with oregano and other spices. In the province of Pampanga, it is stuffed with a mixture of rice and oregano. Lemon grass is used in some parts of the Visayas. In its more elaborate form, lechon is stuffed with paella, a saffron-flavored stew made of green peas, shrimp, crab, and chorizo, or pork sausage.

Despite the different ways lechons are marinated, the taste of the meat does not vary significantly. Strikingly different, however, are the accompanying sauces. Such sauces are usually liver-based and either sweet and sour or spicy. Every person who makes lechon, however, likes to come up with a sauce that is unique, mixing the basic ingredients of vinegar, salt, and sugar with his or her own favorite herbs and spices.

Endangered Species

Philippine Eagle

Also known as the monkey-eating eagle, the Philippine eagle has brown feathers and stands at a height of about 3 feet (0.9 m). Its wings stretch well beyond 8 feet (2.4 m). Philippine eagles are an endangered species, and the Philippine Eagle Conservation Foundation was established in 1980 to prevent their extinction. In 1992, for the first time, a Philippine eagle, named *Pagasa*, or Hope, was born in captivity. By February 1999, a third eagle, the first to be conceived naturally, was born. Previously, the eagles were bred by artificial insemination because Philippine eagles are so choosy about their mates; they often prefer the companionship of their full-time human caretakers.

Above: **The Sulu Archipelago is a sanctuary for Philippine turtles.**

Sea Cows

Sea cows, or dugongs, are also endangered animals. They are the only Indo-Pacific sirenians, or herbivorous sea mammals, still living today. While some are hunted for their meat, most of these gentle creatures are caught by accident in fishing nets and die. Increasing urbanization and industrialization have also destroyed many of their natural habitats. Dugongs eat leaves, roots, and sea-grass. A dugong calf is breast-fed for about eighteen months, and it stays with its mother until a new calf is born.

Left: **This Philippine eagle displays its affection for its caretaker.**

Sea Turtles

Only eight species of sea turtles are known to inhabit Earth, and five are found in Philippine waters: the green sea turtle, the hawksbill, the loggerhead, the Pacific ridley, and the leatherback. The green sea turtle lays its eggs on the Turtle Islands, about 620 miles (1,000 km) south of Manila. Coastal development and illegal hunting of turtle eggs adversely affect the existing turtle population. Also, a high demand for turtle by-products, such as decor and jewelry pieces, encourage poachers to violate environmental laws.

Coral Reefs

At least 488 of the 500 coral species in the world are found in the Philippines. Nevertheless, the country's coral reefs are declining because of increasing trawl-net fishing and land erosion. In addition, coastal deforestation and poor agricultural practices cause large amounts of sediment to be washed onto the reefs, damaging or killing the coral. Thirty percent of Philippine reefs are reportedly dead, while another 39 percent are dying.

Above: **The number of dugongs found in Philippine waters is so small that it makes this sighting of a dugong basking in the sun rare and precious.**

An Ethnic Minority

Muslim Mindanao

The Muslims of the Mindanao region, also known as Moros, are the largest cultural minority in the Philippines. They consider the island of Mindanao and the Sulu Archipelago their "Moroland," and they have continually fought for political autonomy. In 1996, the Moro National Liberation Front (MNLF), the largest Muslim rebel group at that time, signed a peace agreement with the Philippine government, ending decades of violent clashes between them. The agreement also brought about the formation of a special autonomous region, consisting of four provinces in the southern Philippines — Lanao del Sur, Maguindanao, Sulu, and Tawitawi.

Muslims in Mindanao can be divided into five major subgroups: Tausug, Maranao, Maguindanao, Samal, and Badjao. The Tausugs were the first group to adopt Islam, and they ruled

OTHER MUSLIM REBEL GROUPS

The Moro Islamic Liberation Front (MILF), was the second-largest rebel group, with about 20,000 members, until MNLF, which had almost 60,000 members, agreed to a ceasefire in 1996. The Abu Sayyaf is a small but high-profile terrorist group. They have about 500 followers and have been active for ten years.

Below: This typical modern-day Moro couple lives in the southern Philippines.

54

ancient Jolo. Today, the Tausugs reside on the main island of Jolo and around the port of Zamboanga.

The Maranaos live along Lake Sultan Alonto, also known as Lake Lanao. They were the last of the five groups to accept Islam. The Maranao are skilled woodcarvers who make beautiful decorative artifacts. They also make good-quality brassware.

The Maguindanaos are the largest group of Filipino Muslims. They live in the provinces of North and South Cotabato, which experience volatile weather. Their land is periodically flooded by water from overflowing rivers. Given this adverse condition, the Manguindanaos face greater economic obstacles than other tribes. They hunt and grow crops for food in addition to selling woven mats and baskets for a living.

The Samals are the poorest of all the Mindanao Muslim groups. Their lives are completely sea-oriented, and they live in villages built on stilts over the coastal waters. They weave bright and colorful mats that are very popular with urban Filipinos.

The Badjaos are a community of sea-gypsies. Very little is known about them except that they live in their tiny craft their entire lives, and many have tawny complexions and pale hair.

Famous Filipino Painters

In the nineteenth century, a high demand existed for portraits and other types of paintings to decorate the homes of wealthy Spaniards and Filipinos. The first Filipino painter to become famous was Damian Domingo. He is known for his nineteenth-century portraits of Manila residents in their native costumes. Toward the end of that century, two Filipino painters — Juan Luna and Felix Hidalgo — won prizes at the Exposición Nacional de Bellas Artes, a prestigious art competition held in Madrid, Spain, every three years.

Above: **Juan Luna painted this untitled portrait of a lady.**

Juan Luna (1857–1899)

Juan Luna was born in the Philippines on October 23, 1857, and moved to Spain in 1877. In 1881, he became the first Filipino to receive a silver medal at the Madrid exposition, Spain's most prestigious art competition. His winning piece was *Death of Cleopatra*. In 1884, he received a gold medal for *Spoliarium* in the same competition. This painting shows dead Roman gladiators being dragged away. Luna died on December 7, 1899.

Left: **This is Fernando Amorsolo's impression of Ferdinand Magellan's landing on the island of Cebu in 1521.**

Fernando Amorsolo (1892–1972)

In 1972, the same year he died, Fernando Amorsolo became the Philippines' first national artist. Amorsolo was a classicist painter, and the majority of his works were either portraits or landscapes. He used the technique of backlighting, portraying the light in his paintings as coming from behind his subjects. With this method, he created a unique genre of painting characterized by various hues of gold. For popularizing this technique, he was called "the discoverer of Philippine sunlight."

Vicente Manansala (1910–1981)

Vicente Manansala was declared a national artist in 1981. While his paintings are generally more romantic, his critics labeled him a cubist. It was Manansala's technique of using colors to disguise an unrelieved and somber sense of anxiety in his paintings that made them reminiscent of romanticism. Manansala's works are spectacular because they show how he skillfully retained a native touch while utilizing modern techniques. *Fishes* and *Carabaos* are two of Manansala's more famous oil paintings.

Above: **This is Fernando Amorsolo's *First Baptism*, which is his impression of the first baptism ever held in the Philippines.**

Historic City of Manila

Manila is the capital city of the Philippines and one of the oldest cities in the country. Over ten million people live in Manila. The name *Manila* evolved from the words *may nilad* (may NEE-lahd), which means "where the nilad grow." The nilad is a flower that used to grow in that particular area of the Philippines.

In 1571, the Spanish explorer Miguel López de Legazpi founded the city of Manila. Toward the end of the sixteenth century, the Spanish built walls around a large portion of the city because they were afraid of being invaded, especially by the Muslims from the southern Philippines. This walled city, called Intramuros, resembled a medieval town with moats and drawbridges. In the past, its five gates and drawbridges were closed at night to prevent trespassers from entering the city. Mostly Spaniards resided within the city walls. Other Europeans and Asians lived outside the city in districts such as San Miguel, Quiapo, and Binondo.

Below: **Intramuros is surrounded by several parks. In this park, different types of miniature nipa huts are on display.**

Above: **The designs of newer Philippine buildings are still influenced by the country's old Spanish colonial architecture.**

When the Philippines became an American colony, well-known Chicago architects David Burnham and Pierce Anderson drew up a blueprint for Manila. With their ideas, Manila became an eclectic mix of Spanish, Asian, and modern architecture. The architects did not make major changes to Intramuros because of its historical significance. They did, however, open small portions of the walls to traffic, and the moats were drained, filled, and converted into parks.

Today, only a fraction of the high walls that used to define Intramuros are still standing. Most of these walls were destroyed by the bombings and fighting that took place during World War II. A few historical buildings still exist in Intramuros. They include San Agustin Church, Manila Cathedral, and the ruins of Fort Santiago, a dungeon where the Spaniards once locked up Filipino rebels. The Manila Harbor forms a scenic background to some parts of Intramuros. Chinatown is located just outside Intramuros in the district of Binondo, an area where other Europeans and Asians resided when the country was still a Spanish colony.

Land of Volcanoes

The Philippines is home to some fifty volcanoes, but only ten are active. Some have not erupted in six hundred years. Volcanoes, like typhoons, figure prominently in Philippine life and history.

Mayon Volcano

Standing at approximately 7,943 feet (2,421 m), Mayon in Albay province is the most active Philippine volcano. It has erupted more than forty times in the past four hundred years. Mayon is also characterized by its perfect cone symmetry. Mayon's last major eruption was in February 1814, when it destroyed three towns and covered another two with tons of hot lava, giant rocks, and volcanic ash. Almost 1,600 people died. Today, a church bell tower jutting out of hardened lava is the only reminder of Mayon's destructiveness.

Taal Volcano

At about 1,312 feet (400 m), Taal Volcano may be the smallest volcano in the world, but it is the second most active in the Philippines. Reports say it has erupted more than thirty times in the last five hundred years, and its most violent eruption was in January 1911. Located south of Manila in Batangas province, Taal Volcano is situated in the center of Lake Taal, which is, itself, the crater of a prehistoric volcano. Because of this unique location, Taal Volcano is often called "the volcano within a volcano."

Mount Pinatubo

Mount Pinatubo is on the island of Luzon. Standing at 4,872 feet (1,485 m), it was dormant for 450 years before erupting in 1991. The eruption was one of the most violent in the twentieth century, spewing rock, lava, and ash more than 18.6 miles (30 km) into the sky. It took more than seven hundred lives and injured nearly one million people. Located just 25 miles (40 km) from the summit, Clark Air Base, one of the largest American military stations outside the United States, had to be abandoned. Mount Pinatubo's fury also extended to other countries in the region. Clouds of volcanic ash hovered over Cambodia, Singapore, Indonesia, and Malaysia during the aftermath.

Above: **Many Filipinos still live near Mount Pinatubo despite its eruption in 1991.**

Opposite: **Mayon Volcano last erupted in 1814. The bell tower of Cogsawa Church is the only reminder Filipinos have of that tragedy today.**

May: Month of Festivals

Filipinos host at least one festival or celebration every month, but most of their favorite festivals fall in the month of May.

Flores de Mayo

Flores de Mayo, or the Flowers of May, is the most important of all the May festivals. A grand feast honoring the Virgin Mary is held on the last Sunday of May. The highlight of that day is a procession led by a float of the Virgin Mary. Local women dressed in their best clothes follow the float. Each woman carries a flower as tribute to the Virgin Mary.

Left: **On the island of Panay, a beauty pageant is part of the Flores de Mayo celebrations. Here, a contestant is being escorted onto the stage.**

Santacruzan

Santacruzan, or the festival of the Holy Cross, is a nine-day event honoring the Holy Cross of Jesus. Legend has it that Queen Helena, mother of Roman Emperor Constantine, found the cross on which Jesus was crucified and moved it to Rome. The legend is remembered in the climax of the Santacruzan, a procession in which young women are dressed as biblical characters. Some women dress as the Virgin Mary, and younger girls dress as angels. The main character of the procession is Queen Helena. She is followed by a boy who portrays the young Constantine.

Above: **These villagers on the southern part of Luzon, just outside the province of Quezon, are celebrating Pahiyas.**

Pahiyas

Pahiyas falls on the fifteenth day of May and is celebrated mainly by the agricultural communities of Quezon, a province on Luzon. On Pahiyas, or the Feast of San Isidro, Filipinos thank God for the past harvest and seek his blessings for the next planting season. The patron saint of the occasion is San Isidro Labrador, who was a farmer from a town near Madrid, Spain. A statue of him is paraded through the streets, while families showcase the best of their last harvest outside their homes. The display of each family reflects its occupation, so the town's baker puts out his best bread, while farmers display their best fruits or vegetables.

National Attire

The barong tagalog and the *terno* (tee-AIR-no), national Philippine clothing, evolved through several centuries of foreign rule. Before the Spanish arrived, Filipinos had a style of dressing that indicated a mixture of Malay, Chinese, and Indian influences.

Barong Tagalog

During Spanish rule, Filipino men had to wear shirts that were untucked so they could be distinguished from the Spaniards. Not even the mestizos, the elite at that time, were allowed to tuck their shirts into their trousers. The Filipinos then turned the untucked shirt into a unique classic — the barong tagalog, a collared, long-sleeved shirt that ends its shirttail with straight, horizontal seams.

The early version of the barong tagalog was worn with a silk belt, and either the shirt or the belt was dyed red, a color favored by the Filipinos because it symbolized bravery.

Today, the barong tagalog is simply worn with a pair of dark pants. It is usually made either of pina, a cloth woven from pineapple fibers, or a kind of silk known as jusi. It is also exquisitely embroidered. While the traditional barong tagalog came only in white or off-white colors, recent fashion trends have reintroduced it in a variety of colors.

Left: **These two wedding guests have donned the traditional barong tagalog for the special occasion.**

Terno

Unlike the barong tagalog, the national costume for Filipino women, the terno, was not politically inspired. Instead, it evolved from the *camisa* (cah-MEE-sah), a collarless, long-sleeved blouse, and the *saya* (SAH-yah), a long skirt. *Terno*, means "matched" in Spanish, and a terno is simply a combination of a camisa and a saya that have been made of matching fabric.

At the turn of the nineteenth century, the camisa and the saya evolved into a style that incorporated Spanish and Victorian elements. The resulting dress was known as "Maria Clara," named after the submissive heroine of the novel *Noli Me Tangere* by Dr. José Rizal. The saya used to be worn only in rural areas, but the upper class adopted it, widening the skirts and making them in satin or brocade. The camisa, similarly, became more dramatic. Wide sleeves billowed from the shoulders to cover the arm. These sleeves were the origins of the now famous "butterfly" sleeves found on today's ternos.

Above: **Dancing in their best ternos, these women add color and an air of festivity to the party.**

Philippine Churches

More than three hundred years of Spanish rule has left the Philippines with some of the finest church architecture outside Europe. The European Renaissance heavily influenced the style of its Roman Catholic churches, which have walls about 3 to 6 feet (1 to 2 m) thick. Philippine churches, though old, are rarely empty. Masses are held every day of the week, and congregations fill the churches on Sundays.

San Agustin Church, Manila

San Agustin, the oldest Philippine church, was built between 1587 and 1607 by a Spaniard named Juan Marcias. The church survived the 1898 Philippine revolution against Spain, World War II, and even several earthquakes. The earthquake in 1880, in particular, damaged one of the church's twin towers, which had to be dismantled. The tower's removal was the church's only major structural change. The church has twelve uniquely styled chapels, and the carved images of Saints Augustine and Monica on its massive door remain visible today.

Below: **The interior of San Agustin Church is filled with elaborate details, reflecting the Baroque style of architecture common in old Spanish buildings.**

Barasoain Church, Bulacan Province

Barasoain Church began as a wooden church in 1859. Between 1871 and 1878, a stone church was built to replace the wooden structure, but it was destroyed by the 1880 earthquake. In 1885, Father Juan Giron hired a builder to restore the church from the ground up. In 1898, the first Philippine Constitution was drafted in this church. Joseph Estrada, the nation's thirteenth president, was sworn in here exactly one hundred years later.

Las Piñas Church, Manila

Las Piñas Church took nine years (1810–1819) for prison inmates who had been sentenced to hard labor to build it. The church also houses the only bamboo organ of its kind in the world. Friar Diego de Cera built the organ in 1823, modeling it after sixteenth-century Spanish organs. The organ was not used for a time, however, and fell into disrepair. In 1973, it was shipped to Germany to be restored. Today, its beautiful sounds are heard regularly in the church.

Above: **Made of bamboo, this sixteenth-century organ is the only one of its kind in the world. Its unique sounds echo inside Las Piñas Church.**

Sabong: King of Sports

After basketball, sabong, or cockfighting, is the second most popular sport in the Philippines. Deeply enmeshed in Philippine culture, the sport existed even before the Spanish arrived and has survived throughout the centuries despite all attempts to ban it. The sport has faced strong opposition from the Catholic Church, which specifically opposes the gambling that sabong involves. Although the Philippine government has legalized the fights, the law requires that the fights be held only on Sundays and public holidays and that they be situated away from schools, churches, hospitals, and government buildings.

Sabungan (sah-boon-YUN), or cockfighting arenas, throughout the Philippines come alive with every legitimate opportunity. These venues range from small village cockpits, or pens, to massive coliseums that can seat thousands of people. Similar to Roman gladiator competitions, this sport pits two

Below: **In Banaue, cockfight organizers are preparing one of the cockpits for a match as the people around it place their bets.**

roosters against each other until one dies or flees. Sabong begins by matching two roosters according to their weight. A 6-pound (2.7-kg) rooster, for example, fights only other 6-pound roosters. Once the roosters are matched, thin, sharp spurs are attached to the birds' legs. The fight starts with the handlers encouraging the roosters to peck at each other's heads. Once started, the fight continues until one rooster is lying lifeless on the ground or, in some instances, has run away after being wounded. Either way, the referee picks up the winning bird and raises it as a sign of victory.

Spectators can place bets on either the rooster that is favored to win or the one less favored. Stakes in Philippine cockfights range from U.S. $25 to $50. During town fiestas, stakes can go up to $1,000. With such high stakes, it is not surprising that wealthy gamecock lovers are willing to pay exorbitant prices for these roosters, importing them from as far as Texas and London. Most Filipinos, however, raise their own roosters for cockfighting.

In the remote areas of the Philippines, locals are often seen holding their favorite gamecocks under their arms. They are also known to train their roosters extensively at home. Gamecock owners, in general, take exceptional care of their prized birds. The roosters sometimes receive even more attention than the owners' wives and children!

Traditional Games Children Play

Philippine children, especially those in rural areas, still enjoy playing traditional Philippine games. They are inexpensive but are still lots of fun.

Pabitin

The game of *pabitin* (PAH-bee-tihn) is often played during fiestas. Participants grab prizes from a suspended bamboo mesh or from one end of a rope raised and lowered via a pulley that is usually attached to a tree. The prizes may be fruits of the season, moneybags, or candy. To tease the participants, the bamboo mesh is lowered to a height that makes them jump relentlessly. Resourceful participants team up in pairs, and one rides piggyback on the other to reach the prizes. Enterprising ones use a bamboo pole with a hook attached to one end to pick the prizes.

Below: **Filipino children love festivals because they know pabitin is always awaiting them during these special occasions.**

Sungka

When it is raining, children turn to an indoor game called *sungka* (SOONG-kah). Sungka is played on a *sungkahan* (SOONG-kah-HUHN), a wooden board that has sixteen circular holes. Each of the two large holes at either end is called an *ulo* (OO-loh), or "head," and each of the fourteen small holes is called a bahay, or "house." Each of the two players is allocated seven houses on one side and one head. The game pieces, or tokens, are usually shells, pebbles, or seeds.

The object of the game is to accumulate as many tokens as possible in the head. The game begins with forty-nine tokens equally distributed to alternate houses, so that every other hole has seven tokens. The first player starts from the house on the extreme left of his or her side, collects the tokens from the first hole, and drops a token into each hole to the right until there are no more tokens left. The player collects all the tokens in the hole where the last token falls, and then proceeds to distribute them in the same way. The player ends a turn when he or she drops the last token into an empty house. The other player then chooses which house he or she wishes to start from, collects all the tokens there, and distributes them. If the last token falls into an empty house that is opposite one with tokens, the player can collect all the tokens in that house and put them in his or her ulo.

Unique Philippine Transportation

Jeepney — King of the Road

The jeepney is evidence of Philippine innovation. After World War II, Filipinos transformed jeeps left behind by the U.S. Army into a gaily decorated mode of public transportation. Painted in vivid colors and patterns, jeepneys are also decked with mirrors, religious icons, and multicolored lights.

The jeepney has a less well-known cousin — the stainless steel jeep. In 1971, the first stainless steel jeep was produced by metalworker Tomas Araga for practical reasons; fishermen in that area had complained that seawater was corroding their jeepneys. While it costs twice as much as an ordinary jeep, the stainless steel jeep requires less maintenance because it does not rust, and it is difficult to dent. Fishermen, jeepney operators, and even the wealthy began buying stainless steel jeeps because they are adapted to counter the unique Philippine climate, specifically briny air from the surrounding seas and harsh, erratic weather.

Above: **Jeepneys are frequently seen on the streets of Manila. They operate as minibuses, taking paying customers wherever they want to go.**

Banca — Gliding Through the Sea

The *banca* (BUNG-kah) is a narrow wooden boat that usually has an outboard motor attached to the back. Unlike conventional motorboats, which are wider and heavier, bancas are designed to glide across the water. They have wooden frames extending from either side of the boat that function like pontoons, preventing the boat from tipping over or capsizing.

The first bancas were used before the Spanish arrived in 1521. Early Filipinos used them to facilitate trade among neighboring islands. In those days, before outboard motors were invented, paddles were used to move the boats across water. Sails were

Below: **Bancas serve as water taxis, ferrying passengers from island to island.**

never used — and still are not used today — because of the rough, unpredictable monsoon weather.

Bancas are a popular mode of transportation for both people and goods in the Philippines. For a country made up of more than 7,100 islands, jeepneys and other forms of land transportation are hardly adequate for Filipinos to get from one part of the country to another. While most of the country's major islands are equipped for air travel, traveling by bancas is far more affordable. Today, fishermen, pearl divers, and seashell collectors, in particular, rely heavily on bancas for their livelihood.

RELATIONS WITH NORTH AMERICA

The United States and Canada are two of the Philippines' closest allies outside Asia. Historically, diplomatic ties between the three countries developed from a shared belief that every society should be democratic and free. Citizens of the Philippines and the United States, in particular, joined forces in both World War II and the Vietnam War to defend this common ideal. Canada has focused on reducing poverty in the Philippines with extensive funding and trade. Geographically, the three nations are linked by the Pacific Ocean, and advancing communication and transportation technologies have only strengthened the trade relations between the Philippines and North America.

With such strong diplomatic and economic ties, it is not surprising that more and more Filipinos are migrating to the United States and Canada. Over one million Filipinos already live in the United States, and more than four hundred thousand Filipinos live in Canada. Some of these immigrants have made outstanding contributions to their new homelands in North America.

Opposite: U.S. sailors perform a final flag ceremony at Subic Bay Naval Base in 1991.

Below: U.S. president Bill Clinton (*second from right*) and Philippine president Joseph Estrada (*far left*) shake hands at the end of an Asia-Pacific Economic Cooperation (APEC) meeting in Auckland, New Zealand, in 1999.

Ties with the United States

The United States and the Philippines have maintained over one hundred years of special ties since the turn of the twentieth century, when the Philippines became a U.S. colony. For almost five decades, the Philippines and the United States helped establish a Philippine education system, congress, and government. In July 1946, the Philippines gained independence from the United States. Ties between the two countries, however, remained strong, especially when it came to the military.

For decades, the Philippine army was supported by the U.S. armed forces under the Military Bases Agreement (MBA). Before they were closed, Clark Air Base and Subic Bay Naval Base were the two largest American military stations outside the United States. In 1991, Philippine lawmakers rejected a new treaty. This rejection forced the U.S. military to withdraw all its facilities from the Philippines. Despite the departure of the U.S. military, the Mutual Defense Treaty of 1951 continues to be the legal basis for many joint military exercises between the Philippines and the United States armed services today.

Below: **U.S. sailors disembark at Subic Bay Naval Base in the Philippines before its closure in 1991.**

Ties with Canada

In 1999, the Philippines and Canada marked the fiftieth
anniversary of diplomatic ties between the two countries. Both
have built a solid record of cooperation in organizations, such as
the United Nations, the Asia-Pacific Economic Cooperation
(APEC), and the Association of Southeast Asian Nations (ASEAN).

Since the 1970s, the Canadian International Development
Agency (CIDA) has aided community-based development in the
Philippines. Its support peaked after the bloodless People Power
Revolution in February 1986, when the Canadian government
prioritized its assistance to the Philippines over other countries,
with projects designed to relieve women and children in poor
communities, protect the environment, and improve
Philippine telecommunications.

Since the start of diplomatic ties, the Canadian naval and
air forces have frequently visited the Philippines. Apart from
performing military exercises, they have repaired orphanages
and flown relief supplies to Philippine typhoon victims in an
attempt to promote goodwill and friendship.

Above: **Canadian prime
minister Jean Chrétien
and his wife receive
military honors during
their three-day visit to
Manila in 1997.**

Philippine–U.S. Relations Today

The relationship between the Philippines and the United States is founded on equality and mutual respect. The United States has an active foreign policy toward the Philippines that encourages mutual trade. The United States has also pursued similar trade plans with other countries in Asia.

Half the world's population lives in Asia, and Asians produce goods and services that amount to half the global economy. The Philippines and its neighboring countries are not only important suppliers of goods needed in the United States, they also form a large market for American products.

In 1995, the Philippines imported about U.S. $5 billion in American goods and exported over U.S. $6 billion to the United States, making the latter the largest market for Philippine goods. The volume of trade between the two countries continued to increase until 1997. From 1997 to 1998, the Asian economic crisis crippled the Philippine economy, reducing the country's ability to import goods from the United States and other trading partners.

Left: **Athletic shoes are one of the many American products imported by the Philippines. They are, however, very expensive. Philippine college students cannot always afford new pairs, so they take their old ones to shoe repairers like Romy Cruz (*left*), who restores them for approximately U.S. $5.**

American businesses rank among the top foreign investors in the Philippines. Apart from large corporations such as Dole and Del Monte, hundreds of smaller American companies are currently working in various sectors of the Philippine economy. Some companies are improving the country's power supply and its telecommunication services, while others are developing its electronic and manufacturing sectors. American firms looking to operate in the Philippines always will have an advantage over their international competitors because of the many friendships that were forged when the Philippines was a U.S. colony and when the United States maintained its naval and air force bases in the country.

Above: **Some large U.S. businesses have shops in the streets of Manila.**

The Philippines is also one of the five core allies the United States has in the Asia-Pacific region — along with South Korea, Australia, Japan, and Thailand. In 1999, the Estrada government approved a Visiting Forces Agreement (VFA) with the United States, reinforcing the already strong military links between the two countries.

Philippine–Canadian Relations Today

Although diplomatic ties between the Philippines and Canada were established in 1949, relations between the two countries flourished only after Corazon Aquino became president of the Philippines in 1986. Since then, trade between Canada and the Philippines has more than tripled, reaching U.S. $578 million in 1993. Canada is the fifteenth-largest investor in the Philippines, with funding amounting to approximately U.S. $90 million. Major Canadian investors include Sun Life of Canada, the Bank of Nova Scotia, Placer Dome, and BC Packers.

The number of Canadian companies in the Philippines increased significantly in the 1990s. Today, over thirty Canadian businesses have resident offices in the Philippines, and more than seventy firms run their businesses from Canada via partners and agents in the Philippines. These firms are usually engaged in financial services, information technology, agriculture, and food processing. As a result of trade deals, Filipinos have been exposed to a wide range of Canadian produce, ranging from apples and canola oil to aerospace and defense equipment.

Left: Canadian prime minister Jean Chrétien (*left*) and former Philippine president Fidel Ramos (*right*) stand before an applauding audience after signing a Can $2.2 billion trade deal.

When Fidel Ramos succeeded Aquino as president of the Philippines, the volume of trade between the two countries rose sharply again, reaching U.S. $826 million in 1995 — a sixfold increase compared to 1985. Today, the Philippines imports mostly cereals, ores, zinc, and machinery from Canada. The bulk of its exports, in return, are electronic goods or their components, bedding, clothing, and paper.

Canada's relationship with the Philippines is also marked by many humanitarian projects and causes. To support Philippine president Joseph Estrada's development agenda, Canada has given grants totaling U.S. $25 million to help reduce poverty in the Philippines, with a focus on Mindanao and the islands in western Visayas. The latter consists of the central portion of the Philippine Archipelago.

In the 1990s, the Canada-ASEAN Governance Innovations Network (CAGIN) implemented two major projects in the Philippines with the help of the Canadian International Development Agency (CIDA). One was a solid-waste management project on Inampulugan Island in the Iloilo province, and the other was the Eco-Walk Environmental Awareness program for children in the city of Baguio.

Above: **In 1998, members of CAGIN organized the Eco-Walk Awareness program for children of the city of Baguio.**

Early Immigrants: Crew Members and Cabin Attendants

The migration of Filipinos to the United States started as early as the sixteenth century. Philippine seamen who left the services of Spanish ships settled in either the marshes of Louisiana or the coastal towns of Acapulco, Mexico. These Manilamen, as they were called, were then joined by Filipinos who were crew members of Canadian and American ships that were en route to British Columbia and Alaska for trading and whaling expeditions. These Filipinos tended to settle on the west coast of the United States and Canada. Cabin attendants and deckhands who had served on American and European passenger ships stayed mostly in New York and worked in hotels and restaurants.

Filipino Laborers (1900s–1940s)

By the turn of the century, the United States had come to be known as a haven for those seeking political, social, and economic refuge. This reputation attracted scores of Filipinos to the United States shortly after the Philippines became an American colony in 1898. In the same era, an increasing demand for U.S. agricultural products globally led to a major labor shortage in the United States. Filipinos, mainly from northern Luzon, arrived by the

Below: **Filipinos perform in front of the San Francisco Museum of Modern Art as part of the 1999 Philippine-American Arts Festival.**

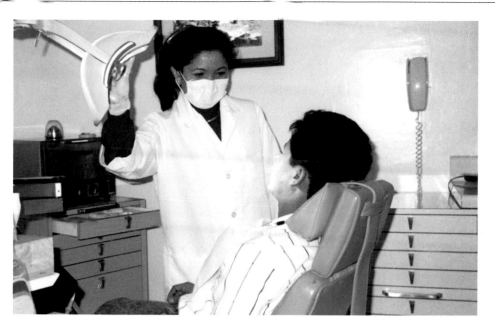

Left: **Dr. Prescilla Molingit, a Filipino-American dentist, examines a patient. She is based in Los Angeles, California.**

thousands to meet that shortage, working in sugar and pineapple plantations in Hawaii, as well as in fruit and vegetable orchards in California and Washington. Some went as far as Alaska to work in fish canneries. The first Filipino to migrate to Canada arrived in 1931. In the three decades that followed, the number of Filipino immigrants in Canada remained insubstantial.

Professionals and Their Families (1950s–1990s)

The most recent wave of Filipinos migrating to North America started after World War II. These Filipinos were mainly World War II veterans who preferred working in the United States, as opposed to staying in postwar Philippines. Apart from veterans, Philippine professionals, such as physicians, nurses, engineers, and businessmen, also migrated to the United States. An immigration reform law in 1965, which encouraged lone immigrants to be reunited with their families, drew even more Filipinos to the United States. Over one million Filipinos live in the United States today.

In the early 1970s, the dictatorial policies of President Ferdinand Marcos caused many Philippine professionals, especially doctors, nurses, and laboratory technicians, to explore the growing opportunities in Canada. These Filipinos eventually settled in Canada's major cities of Winnipeg, Vancouver, Toronto, and Montreal. Today, over four hundred thousand Filipinos live in Canada.

Left: **Victoria Manalo Draves, Filipino-American and Olympic gold medalist (*right*), congratulates a fellow diver on his gold medal.**

Filipinos and Their Influence

The influence of the United States on the Philippines is obvious, from political institutions patterned after their counterparts in the United States to the American fast food Filipinos love. Philippine influence on the United States, however, is not so apparent. Filipinos are the fastest growing group of Asian immigrants in the United States, and Los Angeles, California, is the U.S. city with the largest number of Filipinos. Philippine food, movies, music, dances, newspapers, magazines, clothes, books, and art are available throughout the United States, especially in California, New York, and Hawaii, where large Filipino communities exist. Bataan, Manila, and Corregidor are street names in the United States, and universities offer courses on Philippine history, culture, politics, government, and languages.

The yo-yo, something so often associated with American culture, was actually a deadly weapon used during Philippine tribal wars. The weapon was brought to the United States and converted into a toy by Pedro Flores, an inventor who arrived in the United States in the 1920s.

Some outstanding Philippine athletes have made their marks in U.S. sporting history. Bobby Balcena (1925–1990) played major league baseball for the Cincinnati Reds in 1956. He was born in San Pedro, California, to Filipino immigrant parents. At the 1948 Olympics in London, Victoria Manalo Draves (1924–) represented the United States and dazzled the world by becoming the first woman in Olympic history to win gold medals in both springboard and platform diving in the same competition.

Many Philippine authors are published in the United States. José Garcia Villa (1908–1997), for example, was the author of *Have Come, Am Here* and *Selected Poems and New*. He had resided in New York, where he had lived since the 1930s. Also based in New York is poet and novelist Jessica Hagedorn (1949–). Her first novel was nominated for the National Book Award in 1990. Carlos Bulosan (1911–1956) wrote for *The New Yorker*. He was also the author of *Voice of Bataan*, *The Laughter of My Father*, *America Is in the Heart*, and *Power of the People*. Nestor Vincente Madali Gonzalez (1915–1999) was formerly a professor of English at California State University, Hayward. He was a well-known novelist and short story writer, and his works include *Seven Hills Away*, *Children of the Ash Covered Loam and Other Stories*, and *Look*.

Filipino-Canadians are known, in particular, for their contribution to the health care sector of Canada. At least one person of Filipino descent works in every hospital in Canada. Several Filipino doctors have gained prominence as specialists in their fields.

Below: **Emil Guillermo (1955–), the first Filipino-American and also the first Asian-American to be a regular host on National Public Radio, answers questions about his latest book, *AMOK*.**

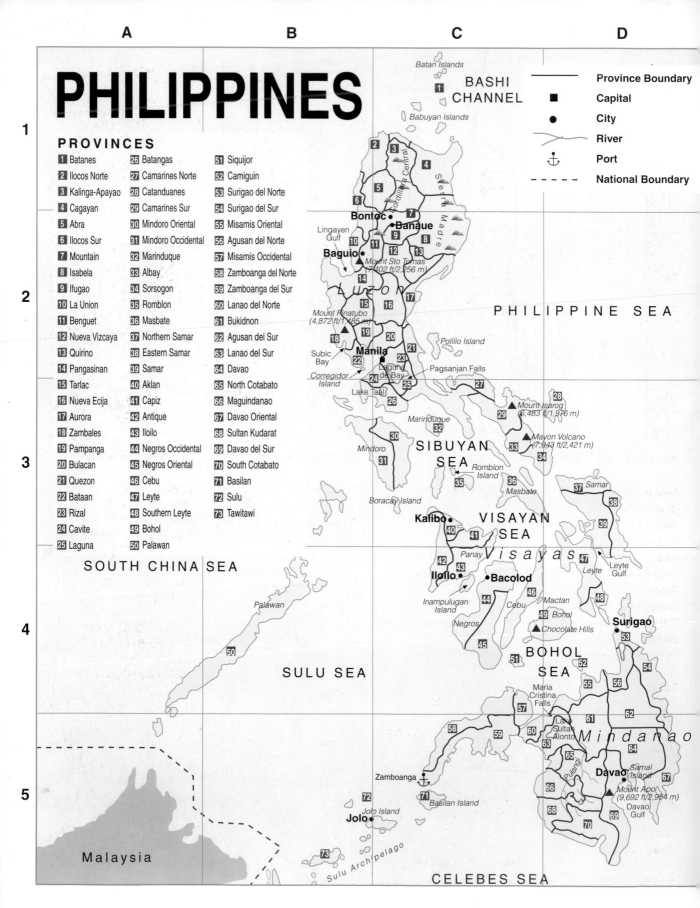

PHILIPPINES

PROVINCES

1 Batanes	**26** Batangas	**51** Siquijor
2 Ilocos Norte	**27** Camarines Norte	**52** Camiguin
3 Kalinga-Apayao	**28** Catanduanes	**53** Surigao del Norte
4 Cagayan	**29** Camarines Sur	**54** Surigao del Sur
5 Abra	**30** Mindoro Oriental	**55** Misamis Oriental
6 Ilocos Sur	**31** Mindoro Occidental	**56** Agusan del Norte
7 Mountain	**32** Marinduque	**57** Misamis Occidental
8 Isabela	**33** Albay	**58** Zamboanga del Norte
9 Ifugao	**34** Sorsogon	**59** Zamboanga del Sur
10 La Union	**35** Romblon	**60** Lanao del Norte
11 Benguet	**36** Masbate	**61** Bukidnon
12 Nueva Vizcaya	**37** Northern Samar	**62** Agusan del Sur
13 Quirino	**38** Eastern Samar	**63** Lanao del Sur
14 Pangasinan	**39** Samar	**64** Davao
15 Tarlac	**40** Aklan	**65** North Cotabato
16 Nueva Ecija	**41** Capiz	**66** Maguindanao
17 Aurora	**42** Antique	**67** Davao Oriental
18 Zambales	**43** Iloilo	**68** Sultan Kudarat
19 Pampanga	**44** Negros Occidental	**69** Davao del Sur
20 Bulacan	**45** Negros Oriental	**70** South Cotabato
21 Quezon	**46** Cebu	**71** Basilan
22 Bataan	**47** Leyte	**72** Sulu
23 Rizal	**48** Southern Leyte	**73** Tawitawi
24 Cavite	**49** Bohol	
25 Laguna	**50** Palawan	

Legend:
- Province Boundary
- ■ Capital
- ● City
- River
- ⚓ Port
- National Boundary

SOUTH CHINA SEA

BASHI CHANNEL

Batan Islands

Babuyan Islands

PHILIPPINE SEA

Bontoc
Banaue
Baguio

Lingayen Gulf

Mount Sto Tomas (7,402 ft/2,256 m)

LUZON

Mount Pinatubo (4,872 ft/1,485 m)

Subic Bay

Manila

Corregidor Island

Laguna de Bay

Lake Taal

Subic Bay

Polillo Island

Pagsanjan Falls

Mount Isarog (6,483 ft/1,976 m)

Marinduque

Mayon Volcano (7,943 ft/2,421 m)

SIBUYAN SEA

Mindoro

Romblon Island

Masbate

Samar

Boracay Island

Kalibo

VISAYAN SEA

V i s a y a s

Panay

Leyte

Leyte Gulf

Iloilo

Bacolod

Inampulugan Island

Cebu

Mactan

Negros

Bohol

▲ *Chocolate Hills*

Surigao

BOHOL SEA

SULU SEA

Palawan

Maria Cristina Falls

Mindanao

Lake Sultan Alonto

Zamboanga ⚓

Pulangi

Davao

Samal Island

▲ *Mount Apo (9,692 ft/2,954 m)*

Davao Gulf

Basilan Island

Jolo

Jolo Island

Sulu Archipelago

CELEBES SEA

Malaysia

86

Above: A traditional form of public transportation, pedicabs are still popular on the island of Leyte.

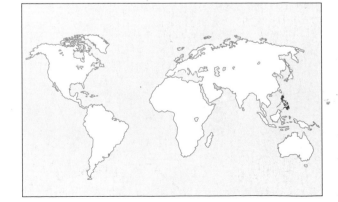

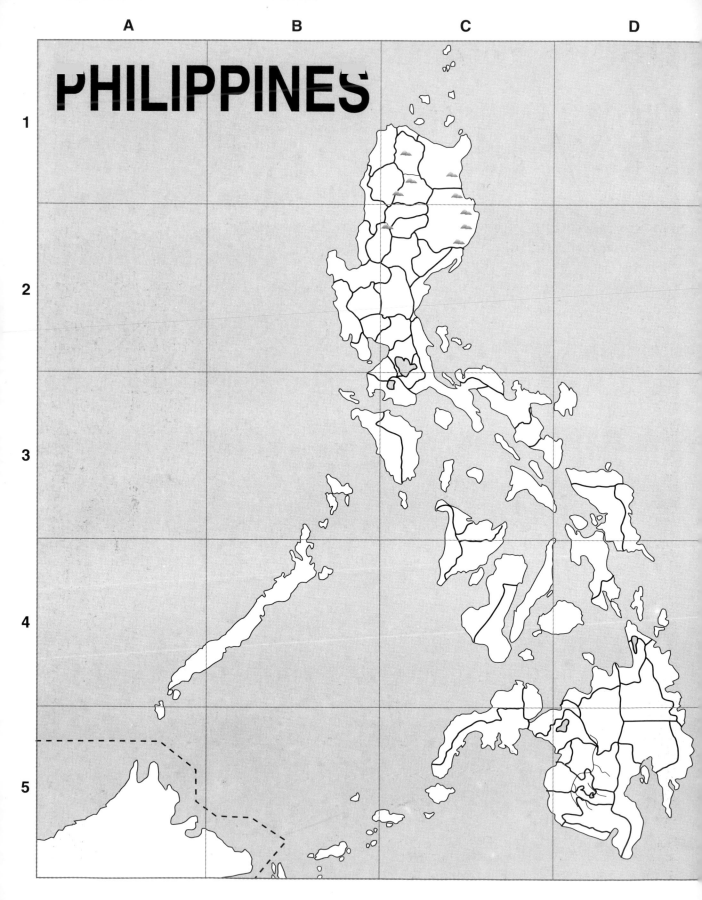

PHILIPPINES

How Is Your Geography?

Learning to identify the main geographical areas and points of a country can be challenging. Although it may seem difficult at first to memorize the locations and spellings of major cities or the names of mountain ranges, rivers, deserts, lakes, and other prominent physical features, the end result of this effort can be very rewarding. Places you previously did not know existed will suddenly come to life when referred to in world news, whether in newspapers, television reports, or other books and reference sources. This knowledge will make you feel a bit closer to the rest of the world, with its fascinating variety of cultures and physical geography.

Used in a classroom setting, the instructor can make duplicates of this map using a copy machine. (PLEASE DO NOT WRITE IN THIS BOOK!) Students can then fill in any requested information on their individual map copies. Used one-on-one, the student can also make copies of the map on a copy machine and use them as a study tool. The student can practice identifying place names and geographical features on his or her own.

Above: **The beach on Boracay Island is especially beautiful at sunset.**

The Philippines at a Glance

Official Name	Republic of the Philippines
Capital	Manila
Official Languages	Pilipino and English
Population	79,345,812 (1999 estimate)
Land Area	115,830 square miles (300,000 square km)
Coastline	22,549 miles (36,289 km)
Provinces	Abra, Agusan del Norte, Agusan del Sur, Aklan, Albay, Antique, Aurora, Basilan, Bataan, Batanes, Batangas, Benguet, Bohol, Bukidnon, Bulacan, Cagayan, Camarines Norte, Camarines Sur, Camiguin, Capiz, Catanduanes, Cavite, Cebu, Davao, Davao del Sur, Davao Oriental, Eastern Samar, Ifugao, Ilocos Norte, Ilocos Sur, Iloilo, Isabela, Kalinga-Apayao, La Union, Laguna, Lanao del Norte, Lanao del Sur, Leyte, Maguindanao, Marinduque, Masbate, Mindoro Occidental, Mindoro Oriental, Misamis Occidental, Misamis Oriental, Mountain, Negros Occidental, Negros Oriental, North Cotabato, Northern Samar, Nueva Ecija, Nueva Vizcaya, Palawan, Pampanga, Pangasinan, Quezon, Quirino, Rizal, Romblon, Samar, Siquijor, Sorsogon, South Cotabato, Southern Leyte, Sultan Kudarat, Sulu, Surigao del Norte, Surigao del Sur, Tarlac, Tawitawi, Zambales, Zamboanga del Norte, Zamboanga del Sur
Highest Point	Mount Apo 9,692 feet (2,954 m)
Major Religion	Roman Catholicism
Current President	Joseph Estrada
Important Holidays	Holy Week (March/April)
	Independence Day (June 12)
	All Saints Day (November 1)
	Christmas (December 25)
Currency	Philippine Peso (44.8 PHP = U.S. $1 as of 2000)

Opposite: **Always clean and colorful, jeepneys are the pride and joy of their owners.**

Glossary

Filipino Words

adobo (AH-doh-boh): pork or chicken marinated in vinegar, soy sauce, garlic, and spices.

amor propio (ah-MOOR pro-PEE-oh): maintaining the dignity of others as well as one's own.

anitos (ah-NEE-tohs): ancestral spirits worshiped by early Filipinos.

anting-anting (UN-ting-UN-ting): a charm that makes its owner invincible against iron weapons.

Ati-Atihan (ah-TEE-AH-tee-hun): annual three-day festival held in Kalibo.

awits (er-WITS): a form of native poetry.

bahay kubo (BAH-hay koo-BOH): hut made of nipa palms and bamboo.

banca (BUNG-kah): a wooden boat.

barangays (bar-RUNG-guys): village communities.

barong tagalog (BAH-rong tah-GAH-lawg): a collared, long-sleeved shirt with shirttails that end in straight, horizontal seams.

bayanihan (BAH-YAH-nee-hun): community spirit.

chicharon (TSEE-tsah-rone): pork crackling.

datus (DAH-toos): village chiefs.

gayuma (gah-YOO-mah): a love potion.

git-git (GEET-geet): a fiddle that uses human hairs for strings.

halo-halo (HAH-loh-HAH-loh): a dessert made of crushed ice, fruit, and milk.

jusi (WHO-see): cloth woven from raw silk threads.

kinilaw (kee-nee-LAW): marinated raw fish.

kudyapi (kood-JAH-pee): a two-stringed instrument that resembles a lute.

kulam (KOO-lum): Philippine voodoo.

kundiman (koon-DEE-mun): a ballad.

lechon (LEHR-tsone): roasted suckling pig.

mañana (MUN-yah-nah): procrastination.

mangkukulam (MUNG-koo-koo-lum): witches.

may nilad (may NEE-lahd): where the nilad, a type of flower, grows; origin of the city name Manila.

mestizos (mis-TEE-sohs): people of mixed Spanish or Chinese and Filipino descent.

moro-moro (MOH-roh-MOH-roh): a literary genre of plays done in verse.

multo (mool-TOH): ghosts.

ningas kogon (NING-us koh-GONE): an inability to stay committed; having a short attention span.

odom (OH-dohm): a magical herb believed to make the people who possess it invisible.

palo sebo (PAH-loh SEE-boh): a traditional game in which the aim is to climb to the top of a greased bamboo pole.

pikon (PEE-con): poor sportsmanship.

pina (PEEN-yah): cloth woven from pineapple fibers.

pulutan (poo-loo-TUN): appetizers.

ramie (RAH-mee): linenlike cloth woven from grass fibers.

sabong (SAH-bong): cockfighting.

sabungan (sah-boon-YUN): pens where cockfighting takes place.

silong (SEE-long): area beneath an elevated nipa hut.

sipa (SEE-pah): to kick; a Philippine game played with a hollow cane ball.

sungkahan (SOONG-kah-HUHN): a wooden game board.

terno (tee-AIR-no): the national costume for Filipino women. It consists of a skirt and a collarless, long-sleeved blouse.

uiga (oo-WEE-gah): a charm that prevents its owner from getting wet.

ulo (OO-loh): head; a hole on a sungkahan.

utung na loob (oo-TUNG nah loh-OHB): repaying favors with intense gratitude.

English Vocabulary

advocated: supported a cause or an idea.

animistic: describing the belief that every part of nature has a spirit or soul.

archipelago: a large group of islands; a large body of water with many islands.

artificial insemination: the injection of seminal fluid into the womb of a female animal by other than natural means.

baroque: a style of art and architecture prominent in the seventeenth century that involves a lot of curved lines and decoration in its design.

ceded: formally granted by treaty.

crucifixion: the act of nailing someone's bound hands and feet to a cross.

cubist: an artist whose style is to reduce natural shapes or forms to their geometrical equivalents.

curricula: the different courses or subject-combinations offered by a school.

despicable: deserving contempt.

dormant: temporarily inactive or not erupting.

eclectic: made up of elements selected from various sources.

fatalistic: describing the belief that events are fixed in advance and that humans are powerless to change them.

impassioned: filled with intense feeling or excitement

kaleidoscope: a constantly changing pattern or scene.

martial law: temporary law and order imposed by state military forces in response to civil unrest.

pagans: people who follow a religion that worships more than one god.

penance: an act performed to show sorrow or repentance for a sin.

perspective: a person's mental view of facts or ideas.

procrastination: the act of delaying to do something.

prolific: highly productive.

propaganda: information that is spread with the purpose of either promoting or damaging a cause or institution

quash: to suppress completely.

romanticism: a style of art and literature that emphasizes the importance of nature, emotion, and imagination.

sedentary: staying in one place, with no plans to migrate.

shingles: rectangular pieces of wood, metal, or other material that are arranged in overlapping rows to cover a roof or sides of a building.

slatting: arranging long, narrow pieces of wood so that they resemble Venetian blinds.

thatch: a covering that is made by stacking materials such as straw or rushes.

More Books to Read

Mga Kuwentong Bayan: Folk Stories from the Philippines. New Faces of Liberty. Alice Lucas, editor (Many Cultures)

On Becoming Filipino: Selected Writings of Carlos Bulosan. Carlos Bulosan and E. San Juan, Jr., editor (Temple University Press)

The People of the Philippines. Celebrating the Peoples and Civilizations of Southeast Asia series. Dolly Brittan (Powerkids Press)

Philippines. Cultures of the World series. Lily Rose R. Tope (Benchmark Books)

The Philippines. Enchantment of the World series. Walter Olesky (Children's Press)

Philippines. Festivals of the World series. Lunita Mendoza (Gareth Stevens)

Philippines. Major World Nations series. Jessie Wee (Chelsea House)

Philippines. Ticket To series. Anne E. Schraff (Carolrhoda Books)

Tales from the 7,000 Isles: Popular Philippine Folktales. Art R. Guillermo (Vision Books International)

When the Rainbow Goddess Wept. Cecilia Manguerra Brainard (University of Michigan Press)

Videos

Best of Nightline: Marcos and Aquino. (MPI Home Video)

José Rizal. (GMA Films)

Philippines. (TMW Media Group)

Philippines: Pearls of the Pacific. (IVN Entertainment)

Web Sites

www.gopinoy.com

www.crosswinds.net/~philipinfo/

lcweb2.loc.gov/frd/cs/phtoc.html

Due to the dynamic nature of the Internet, some web sites stay current longer than others. To find additional web sites, use a reliable search engine with one or more of the following keywords to help you locate information about the Philippines. Keywords: *Maria Corazon Aquino, Filipino, Ifugao, Manila, Ferdinand Marcos, Mindanao, Philippines.*

Index

SVAD 9/18